DISABILITY AND THE ENVIRONMENT

Disability and the Environment

VIDA CARVER and
MICHAEL RODDA

SCHOCKEN BOOKS · NEW YORK

First published by SCHOCKEN BOOKS 1978

Copyright © Elek Books Ltd., 1978

Library of Congress Cataloging in Publication Data

Carver, Vida.
   Disability and the environment.

   Bibliography: p.
   Includes index.
   1. Handicapped.   2.   Architecture and the physically handicapped.   3.   Social   interaction.   4.   Physically   handicapped
services.   I.   Rodda, Michael, joint author.   II.   Title.
HV3000.C37   362.4   78-59602

Manufactured in Great Britain

To
F. Le Gros Clark
and
Boyce R. Williams

'If we could bequeath one precious gift to posterity, I would choose a society in which there is a genuine compassion for the very sick and the disabled, where understanding is unostentatious and sincere; where, if years cannot be added to the lives of the chronically sick, at least life can be added to their years; where the mobility of disabled people is restricted only by the bounds of technical progress and discovery; where the handicapped have the fundamental right to participate in industry and society according to their ability; where socially preventable disease is unknown and where no man has cause to be ill at ease because of his disability.'

ALFRED MORRIS, MP, speaking in the House of Commons during the second reading of his Chronically Sick and Disabled Persons Bill.

Contents

List of Illustrations

List of Tables

Preface

We are most grateful to all those colleagues and friends who in many small and not so small ways have enabled us to write this book. It is not possible to mention all of them by name, but Pat Welch and Carol Welch, our secretaries, have both given generously of their time and Lesley Brazier, Frank Knocker and Fred Brasier have also all been involved in the large number of clerical tasks required in the preparation of the manuscript. Without their help our task would have been so much more difficult.

Dr Rodda was employed by the UK Department of Health and Social Security at the time the text of this book was written. However, the views expressed are entirely his own and do not necessarily reflect the opinions or policies of that Department.

Introduction

Why this book was written

This is not a textbook, although it is hoped that it will be of some value to students of the social and physical environment and of such disciplines as social work, medicine, nursing and psychology which concern themselves with the problems of the individual and his relationship to the world he inhabits. It assumes, however, no prior knowledge of any of these disciplines. Disability is too common a phenomenon in our society to leave it to the experts. There can be very few adults who have not encountered disabled people at work, among their neighbours or in their own families, and, indeed, we are all personally at risk. The issues this book raises are of concern to all of us. Its aims are:

1. To analyse the predicament of disabled people in so far as it arises from their relationship to an environment that has been adapted by many successive generations of unimpaired people to meet the needs of average, able human beings.
2. To examine some of the ways in which the environment might be further adapted to meet a wider range of human needs.
3. To raise questions about the responsibility of individuals, professional and lay, for initiating changes.

The plan of the book

The book falls naturally into three parts. The first two chapters explore in general terms the complex nature of the relationship between disability and environment. In the first, we attempt to define the problem as we see it, clarify some of the concepts in common use and come to terms with ethical implications. In the second we look at more concrete aspects of the relationship: the causes of disability in the modern world, the size of the problem and the associated legislation.

The next four chapters are concerned with the interaction between environment and disability at different ages. In Chapter 3 the physical, perceptual, cognitive and linguistic development of the young unimpaired child are traced as the background for a discussion of the special needs of the impaired child and his family. Chapter 4 deals with children of school age, Chapter 5 with the needs of disabled adults if they are to function as normally as possible as members of the wider community, and Chapter 6 with the complex relationship of ageing and handicap.

The last chapter is entitled 'Looking Ahead' and draws together the implications, as we see them, of the various issues discussed in earlier chapters. We do not attempt to formulate a programme of reform nor do we give detailed consideration to the now wide literature of reports, recommendations and proposals from government departments and special committees on both sides of the Atlantic, and from professional bodies and voluntary organizations concerned with the welfare of various groups of disabled people. Such proposals are usually closely related to the wider political philosophies of those for whom they are prepared, and to the current structure of welfare services in particular countries or even states. In this book we have been more concerned to examine the principles that should inform the direction of change, and even in matters of principle there is not always full agreement among all those sincerely concerned with the need for change. We believe that, since large-scale environmental changes cannot be made in a few months or even a few years, particularly if changes in public attitudes are high in the list of priorities, there is still time for debate before all the options are closed. Nevertheless, this is a personal book which must reflect a personal position. We do not expect the reader always to agree with our conclusions, but we do hope to provide him with the stimulus to think afresh about the issues involved and attempt to define his own position in relation to them.

All the statistical tables reproduced in the text give the latest figures obtainable at the time of publication.

1

What is Disability?

Introduction

Modern man has inherited an environment very different from that of his ancestors. Even the most remote rural communities live in surroundings that have been adapted by successive generations of their predecessors in the interests of more efficient and more satisfying living. Buildings, private and public, provide man with shelter and close community contact with his neighbours; roads and transport systems enable him to widen his horizons and opportunities, and modern technology, through the mass media, makes nearly everyone a potential citizen of the world. Perhaps even more significantly we are born into a network of social institutions which affect every aspect of our daily lives. Government at all levels is an important influence in determining how and where we live and what we may or may not do with our lives. Modern methods of production not only largely determine what we eat and wear, but also provide the structure of choices within which each of us makes his own life and life-style. Educational systems lead us into patterns of thinking which reflect the necessities imposed by the total environment. True, this environment is perpetually changing as we continue to look for even greater satisfactions, but it changes more slowly than the needs of individual man. We are all aware of restrictions imposed by such systems when they become obsolete, and of new opportunities that we as individuals are not yet able to grasp. We continually remake our environment, but at the same time we are to some extent imprisoned by it.

Progress through life can be seen as a succession of interactions with the physical and social environment, which man seeks to adapt at all stages to achieve maximum personal satisfaction. If a man is hungry he may go to a restaurant and order a meal. The waiter (adapting his own behaviour in the interests of holding down his job) serves a well-adapted portion of meat and vegetables, which the hungry man proceeds to eat and digest. He pays the bill and returns to his job—at the coal-face or on the board of directors—for another assault on the environment in the interests of replenishing the reduced contents of his wallet. He is the average man, quietly changing the world around him with little thought about the implications of his actions for others. At best, he may dimly be aware that the six ounces of meat he consumed for lunch may have been produced at the expense of thirty simpler meals for families living near subsistence level in the third world, but what can he do about it? This is his world, as he knows it.

In many ways even further from our consciousness than the third world is the world of the handicapped and the disabled. If our hungry man had been in a wheelchair, the chances are that he would have been unable to enter the restaurant at all because of the three steps leading to the door. If blind, he might have been turned away because social custom makes dogs, including guide dogs, unwelcome in most restaurants. If mentally handicapped, or elderly, he might have been confined to a residential establishment that would not even allow him the opportunity to choose where and what he would like to eat. It is part of our environmental inheritance that the 'normal' environment has been designed in the main by the 'normal' man for the 'normal' man. The twentieth century has witnessed more dramatic changes in the total environment than any comparable recorded period of history. This is due largely to the rapid pace of technological advance, but one of the consequences of this advance has been a rise in the incidence of disability in advanced countries. Greater numbers of severely impaired children are surviving infancy, more people who become sick or are injured in adult life are returned by medical science to the community, more normal adults live long enough to experience the disabilities of old age. Modern technology has preserved their lives and in many cases produced remarkable prosthetics to enable them to continue surviving for many years, but it has also widened the gap between the disabled and the able-bodied in the opportunities given to participate in our common social life. The wider environment, social as well as physical, remains for the most part inflexibly the preserve of the average man.

Defining disability

This book is about some of the handicaps that our largely alien world imposes upon impaired people. 'Impairment', 'disability' and 'handicap' are key concepts in any such discussion. The reader will rightly demand that we should use them with some precision and consistency. Unfortunately the wider literature sets us a poor example. Each term has a long history of imprecise usage and indeed they are often used interchangeably. Some writers appear to regard them as synonymous and distinguish them only in relation to the reader addressed: 'disability' is used as a more polite euphemism for 'impairment', and 'handicap' is the most polite term of the three. There are important issues to be distinguished and this loose kind of usage can only confuse.

There are very real difficulties in the way of reaching precise definitions. One of the assumptions that has to be made by practitioners is that disability can be measured. Most of us can recognize extreme forms of disability but, despite this, disability is a very murky concept in medicine, psychology and sociology. Attempts to define it in absolute terms have always proved easier in theory than in practice. One crucial distinction that must be made is between disability and need. A person may have a very severe disability and yet still have no need of help because he or she has overcome the effects of disability with or without the aid of others. A severely crippled person may have a medically incurable condition and may be properly defined medically as severely disabled. Nevertheless, by providing him with an appropriate wheel-chair, and by adapting his house so that he can undertake normal functions of caring for himself or for others, he may exhibit no social needs in the home environment. When he leaves the house a new set of needs may emerge, concerned with mobility in a larger environment that is not designed to cope with people who are unable to walk normally. Even within the house he may have psychological needs that have not been catered for by the physical adaptations to the environment—he may be bored because he is unable to escape from the confining space of the home, or frustrated because his ability to undertake self-care tasks still does not permit him to do such things as home decorating.

Disability and need are relative terms: the effects of a physical, mental or social condition cannot be defined in the abstract, but can be defined only in relation to individual expectations and individual attributes. Ward (1974) has differentiated these relatives as 'conditions' and 'functions'. A condition is the medical, psychological or social state that is the precipitating event for disability. The function is the adaptation, with or without help, that the individual makes to the precipitating condition. There is no direct relationship between a condition and a function, and the effect of the condition depends upon many other psychological, social and physical factors. We can be reasonably consistent in describing conditions, but our knowledge of functions is more limited and at present most classificatory systems used to describe functions are somewhat less than ideal. Moreover, a psychological condition can influence the social and physical function of the individual, and a medical condition can affect his psychological and social functioning. Inadequacy only results from a state of dependency if we require help in functioning. It does not result from the need for help in dealing with a condition. In the example we gave above, the crippled person needs the help we can provide by making available, whether free or for purchase, a wheelchair and such adaptations to the home as may be necessary for him to follow his familiar patterns of daily living. If through these aids he is able to overcome the effects of the disabling condition his functioning will be adequate and independent.

Since our main concern in this book is the improvement of the quality of life experienced by impaired people, we shall be less concerned with medical classifications and descriptions of disabling conditions, appropriate only to the diagnosis and treatment of disease conditions, than with the functional consequences of disability.

If a man is confined to a wheelchair, knowledge of the cause of his impairment, be it poliomyelitis, spinal injury or a stroke, becomes less important than his aspirations and the particular environmental barriers that stand in the way of their achievement. An example of a classificatory system which emphasizes functions rather than conditions is the one devised by Agerholm (1975) (Table 1). Agerholm defines a handicap as 'a long-term disadvantage which affects an individual's capacity to achieve the personal and economic independence which is normal for his peers'. She further distinguishes between 'extrinsic' and 'intrinsic' handicap as follows:

An extrinsic handicap is such a disadvantage arising from the individual's environment or circumstances (e.g. poverty, material deprivation, racial discrimination, residence in a depressed or disaster area).

An intrinsic handicap is such a disadvantage arising from the individual's own characteristics, from which he cannot be separated.

To illustrate the distinction between an extrinsic and an intrinsic handicap she quotes the Eastern proverb, 'I wept because I had no shoes until I met a man who had no feet'.

TABLE 1

Classification of intrinsic handicaps. (Source: Agerholm, M. 1975. Handicaps and the handicapped: a nomenclature and classification of intrinsic handicaps. *Royal Society of Health Journal*, **95**, 3)

Key handicaps		Handicap components
A Locomotor handicap (the locomotor handicapped)	1	Impaired mobility in environment
	2	Impaired postural mobility (relation of parts of body to one another)
	3	Impaired manual dexterity
	4	Reduced exercise tolerance
B Visual handicap (the visually handicapped)	1	Total loss of sight
	2	Impaired (uncorrectable) visual acuity
	3	Impaired visual field
	4	Perceptual defect
C Communication handicap (the communication handicapped)	1	Impaired hearing
	2	Impaired talking
	3	Impaired reading
	4	Impaired writing

Key handicaps	Handicap components
D Visceral handicap (the viscerally handicapped)	1 Disorders of ingestion 2 Disorders of excretion 3 Artificial openings 4 Dependence on life-saving machines
E Intellectual handicap (the intellectually handicapped)	1 Mental retardation (congenital) 2 Mental retardation (acquired) 3 Loss of learned skills 4 Impaired learning ability 5 Impaired memory 6 Impaired orientation in space or time 7 Impaired consciousness
F Emotional handicap (the emotionally handicapped)	1 Psychoses 2 Neuroses 3 Behaviour disorders 4 Drug disorders (including alcoholism) 5 Antisocial disorders 6 Emotional immaturity
G Invisible handicap (the invisibly handicapped)	1 Metabolic disorders requiring permanent therapy (e.g. diabetes, cystic fibrosis) 2 Epilepsy, and other unpredictable losses of consciousness 3 Special susceptibility to trauma (e.g. haemorrhagic disorders, bone fragility, susceptibility to pressure sores) 4 Intermittent prostrating disorders (e.g. migraine, asthma, vertigo) 5 Causalgia and other severe pain disorders
H Aversive handicap (the aversively handicapped)	1 Unsightly distortion or defect of part of body 2 Unsightly skin disorders and scars 3 Abnormal movements of body (athetosis, tics, grimacing, etc.) 4 Abnormalities causing socially unacceptable smell, sight or sound
J Senescence handicap (the senescence handicapped)	1 Reduced plasticity of senescence 2 Slowing of physical or mental function of senescence 3 Reduced recuperative powers of senescence

The definitions formulated by Harris (1971) in the Social Survey report, *Handicapped and Impaired in Great Britain*, attempted to clear up some of the confusions. They assisted Harris in the production of a useful if limited measuring instrument, a disability scale based upon specific actions which can or cannot be performed in a domestic situation (e.g. getting in and out of bed unaided). These definitions have met with increasing acceptance by workers in the field and for this reason we shall try to keep as closely as we can to her terminology in this book.

Impairment is defined as 'lacking part or all of a limb, or having a defective limb, organ or mechanism of the body'.

Disablement is 'the loss or reduction of functional ability'.

Handicap is 'the disadvantage or restriction of activity caused by disability'.

The reader should, however, keep in mind the preceding discussion and recognize the difficulty in applying these definitions with precision. One needs to be aware, moreover, of hidden values behind their seeming objectivity. In all three there is an implied reference to our old friend the average man, who is the unmentioned norm. Even when constructing definitions we cannot move out of his world.

The implications of these hidden values are important for our discussion. The definitions we use can in themselves help to shape our attitudes. To categorize a person as one who 'lacks' or has 'lost' some part of himself is already to think of him as something less than a complete individual. If we re-wrote 'the reduction of functional ability' as 'the inability to do some or all of those interesting and valuable things that an average man in an average man's world can do' we would be accused of being 'evaluative,' but this reformulation should serve to underline the evaluative implications behind the colder, more abstract terms of the original definition. To be described as disabled or, worse still, as 'one of the disabled', is on either definition to be designated as belonging to a different and probably inferior order of beings. These connotations are well understood, if rarely made explicit, by both disabled and non-disabled people. How else can we explain the estimate by the Department of Employment in Britain (1972) that there are working in industry at least as many disabled people eligible for registration (and the benefits that can accrue from registration) but unwilling to identify themselves as there are registered disabled persons? Or the common but very strange behaviour of most average people who, when they meet a blind person or someone in a wheelchair, will talk to him not directly but through his companion—the phenomenon known to disabled people as the 'Does-your-friend-take-sugar-in-his-tea?' approach. The definition of handicap contains a similar trap. Who decides that the disadvantage or restriction of activity in any particular situation is caused by the disability?

A clerk in a wheelchair may have no handicap in relation to her ability to work, but if she lives in a neighbourhood where most of the offices are above ground-floor level and there are no lifts she is severely handicapped in her ability to find a job. She may be equally handicapped in the most easily accessible office when the potential employer holds generalized and stereotyped attitudes about disability. He may initially perceive her as a substandard human being, rather than as someone fully able to carry out the work for which she is qualified. Handicap, like beauty, may be in the eye of the beholder.

The concept of the impaired person as a whole and complete individual is an important one for the approach we shall be taking in this book. The dissimilarities between even the most severely impaired person and his unimpaired neighbours are far fewer than their similarities. To be human, alive and conscious implies a range of common experiences at the basic tick-over level of physical existence. We are all motivated by essentially the same needs: for food, stimulation, activity and achievement; sex, affectionate relationships and companionship; a stable routine but with some variety and change, and so on. Further, each person impaired or unimpaired experiences himself as a unique individual with particular interests, capabilities and aspirations. In this context, a blind lawyer will feel himself as having more in common with a sighted lawyer than with a blind newsagent. All three are also aware of personal limitations. Both lawyers might have no gift for music, which could be the newsagent's particular interest, but it is a normal human thing to occupy oneself predominantly in areas where one is capable, or at least capable of enjoying learning. In this respect most impaired people, including those whose impairment results in a lower than average level of mental functioning, are as normal as the unimpaired. To be continuously preoccupied with the impossible is more characteristic of the psychiatric patient. All sane human beings seek a meaningful relationship with their environment and people living in a common culture, whatever their abilities or disabilities, pass through similar experiences, learn the same language and customs, and come to share many common ideas and values.

Disability and environment

The relationship of an impaired person to his environment is, however, a particularly complex one. As we have seen, the degree of disability can in some cases be reduced almost to vanishing point by appliances or aids. We may take the example of a good pair of spectacles, so common in the twentieth century that most wearers forget they depend upon them until the day they accidentally break them. For all but a very few jobs, the man wearing glasses is a candidate accepted on equal terms with other applicants. There are even young men who wear glasses with plain lenses to make them appear more mature, but not all aids are as socially acceptable. No one would wear a hearing-aid for cosmetic purposes. Although it may be as important to the wearer as glasses, a hearing-aid has in most cases, like the wheelchair, an immediately stigmatizing effect. The experience of living with stigma is part of the environmental burden of many impaired people. Further, the impaired person is himself a member of society, learning from childhood the very attitudes that reject him along with his disability. Richardson, Hastorf and Dornbusch (1964) made an empirical study of the self-perceptions of 9–11-year-old handicapped and non-handicapped children. They found that already 'the handicapped children are very realistic in their self-descriptions. *Although they share the peer values*, they are aware that they cannot live up to the expectations that stem from the high value placed on physical activities' (our italics). But the handicapped person, child or adult, is not in a position to set himself aside as others may, and many of the problems we have called environmental become personal problems for the disabled. It is professional cant to say simply that a man must 'come to terms with his disability'. What he has to come to terms with is largely what his social environment has made of his disability. This is why our study of the environment must inevitably include the psychological as well as the social problems of impaired people in so far as they relate to their impairment.

There will be less in this book about technology than some readers might expect. The scope of technology is already far in advance of its applications in the field of disability. A great deal of the impairment in the world today could have been prevented, and some could be cured, if greater resources had been available for the application of technological knowledge in the fields of engineering, medicine and surgery. What we are concerned with here, however, is the amelioration of existing disability through environmental adaptation, and the first priority is still to determine what needs to be done now, which we can do in the confidence that the technology is already available that could change the entire quality of life for the majority of disabled people.

As a working definition of *environment* for the purpose of this book, therefore, we offer: the psychological, social and physical aspects of the world surrounding him which may limit or facilitate an impaired person's autonomy.

Rehabilitation

To look at disability as largely an environment problem is of course not a completely new approach. Historically, all those who have sought to alleviate the condition of impaired people have been obliged to effect environmental adaptations. Nineteenth-century philanthropists with their twin devotions to charity and tidiness provided residential schools and sheltered workshops for the blind. While reducing the numbers of beggars on the streets, they effectively segregated the objects of their charity into closed environments away from the wider community. The concept of rehabilitation, as it is understood today, is a product of the twentieth century. It was defined in the Mair Report

(1972) as 'the restoration of patients to their fullest physical, mental and social capacity'. In this comprehensive sense the concept has quite a short history. It took two world wars and, perhaps even more significantly, a labour shortage in the second, to bring central government in Britain and the USA to a realization of the human and economic waste that neglected disability implied. In Britain it was the Minister of Labour who in 1941 appointed the first departmental committee in the UK to review rehabilitation services. The recommendations of this committee (Tomlinson Report, 1943), which became effective through the Disabled Persons (Employment) Act in 1944, determined both the general structure and the philosophy of the rehabilitation services which have remained substantially unchanged until the present day. We may however look forward to some expansion in the provision of rehabilitation facilities in Britain as a consequence of the reorganization of the Employment Service in 1974 and the National Health Service in 1975, even though revolutionary changes in this direction are unlikely.

The rehabilitation model is essentially a medical model designed for crisis intervention. From this spring both its strengths and its shortcomings. The typical war-time rehabilitatee was a young or young-middle-aged male suffering from injuries received in action and still under military discipline at the time of referral. People referred for rehabilitation in the late 1970s are mainly civilians and may be of either sex and any age, and injuries account for only about five per cent of all referrals. The chronic illnesses of middle and old age account for the highest proportion. Impairments of sight and hearing are relatively common; most are gradual in onset, though they may be as severely disabling even in the earlier stages as complete blindness or deafness. People recovering from psychiatric disorders are also frequently referred for rehabilitation.

The first objectives of rehabilitation are the 'restoration' of physical and mental health by means of drugs, remedial exercises, speech- and physio-therapy and re-training in the kind of activities needed for self-care in the home and an early return to work. Aids and appliances may be provided to compensate for loss of function, including artificial limbs, crutches, calipers, wheelchairs and personal aids, and the patient is (or should be) intensively trained in their use. This may be a long and expensive process, involving attention from more than one medical consultant and a number of para-professionals, each a specialist in a different aspect of treatment, who, taken together, constitute the hospital team. When this team has finished its job the patient may be referred (i) to his local social services department for resettlement at home (where some adaptations may be made to the home environment and, if needed, arrangements made for continued nursing and help in home duties), and/or (ii) to the Employment Advisory Service for resettlement in open or sheltered employment, via occupational assessment and/or re-training.

It must be clear that although the focus is firmly on the rehabilitatee with the object of remodelling him as closely as possible to the functional semblance of an average man, rehabilitation is never a simple repair job on a damaged machine. In pursuing the objective of restoring a measure of environmental control many things may well be done to render the environment itself more tractable. These are, however, an extension of the original medical model, although pioneered for the main part by the practitioners themselves who early perceived its limitations.

These limitations were summarized by Warren (1974), as follows:

> Society's attitudes to the handicapped are complex and contradictory. In theory society accepts the handicapped as fellow human beings with the same rights as the able-bodied. In practice, society tends to segregate the handicapped not only in special institutions but also by accepting a stereotype of a handicapped person which tends to set him apart from the able-bodied, by thoughtless lack of design and planning in public and private buildings, and by making 'earning' or housework the only socially acceptable roles for people between leaving school and retirement age. Often society is seeking contradictory objectives to the detriment of the life of the handicapped person and to the frustrations of its own health and social services. What is needed by all with a concern for the disabled and a commitment to rehabilitation is leadership in the efforts to gain acceptance for the disabled in practice and to obtain a quality of life no less satisfactory than that of the able-bodied.

We would argue that the contradiction Warren complains of is reflected in the central conception of rehabilitation. The kind of integration into society that the model implies is simply the old segregation turned upside-down. Both imply a tidying-up operation to keep disabled people and their needs, if not out of sight, out of consciousness—and conscience. Basically, it is a Procrustean model: the man must be fitted to the bed, not the bed to the man. This is not the fault of those who operate the services but of our wider culture which at best only patronizes its minorities. It offers them services, manned by professionals, which are expensive to provide, can never keep up with demand even in a booming economy, and are squeezed and inevitably at risk of being cut back whenever public spending is under pressure.

The services are forced to be selective, in favour of the 'suitable case for treatment' (who may often be identified also as the well-backed, the vociferous, or the lucky). For the rest the support is often minimal. The most suitable cases for rehabilitation are those considered most promising material for eventual return to an unadapted slot in the average scheme of things. It should not be thought that they are necessarily the less severely disabled—who are indeed often passed over by the services and left to struggle on in whatever way they can by themselves. Nor are they the *most* severely disabled who, it is tacitly conceded, are destined to become 'burdens' either to their relatives in their own homes, or to the rate-payer in residential homes. It is therefore necessary to distinguish between *assimilation* or *reassimilation* into an environment essentially unchanged, the prospect offered to the most suitable, and true *integration* which means full membership of society on whatever terms the disabled person can himself offer, as a basic human right. The leadership that Warren calls for should come from disabled people themselves, for they are the people who know what they need, but while they are accorded only second-class citizenship they cannot exercise leadership. It is still only too common for decisions affecting the whole future life-style of a disabled person to be made by a conference of experts while the 'object' of their deliberations sits on a bench outside the door waiting for the answer. High-level committees composed entirely of the non-impaired deliberate the pattern of services to come, the training of personnel, the design of housing, without reference to the potential user. If environments are to accommodate minorities as well as majorities, then we must encourage full participation of minority representatives at all levels where decisions affecting the lives of all people are made. For many disabled people, a life of public service might be the alternative to more conventional occupations than Warren seeks. It would undoubtedly have beneficial results for the community as a whole.

Summary

In this chapter we have attempted to define the main issues with which we shall be concerned in this book. We should also make clear some of the limits we have placed on its scope. We have distinguished between impairment, disability and handicap and between conditions and functions. The definition of impairment we have adopted includes intellectual retardation, but restricts us from the detailed consideration of the disabling effects of psychotic or psychoneurotic disorders which would call for a book to themselves. The main focus of this book is in any case upon functions rather than conditions, and a functional classification of disability is preferred to the medical labels more appropriate for the diagnosis and treatment of disease. This sets the scene for an examination of the many and varied factors in the man-made environment which can either increase or reduce handicap. These include:

1. attitudes of both unimpaired and impaired members of the community;
2. the nature and quality of the services society provides to help meet the difficulties of the impaired;
3. the resources society is prepared to make available for the reduction of handicap, their adequacy or inadequacy, and methods and patterns in resource distribution.

No attempt can be made to evaluate the relative significance of these various factors since they are closely interdependent, but the ways in which they operate together to set limits on the quality of life of impaired individuals is the main theme of this book.

2

The Nature of the Problem

Blind, deaf, physically disabled and many other handicapped people can speak from personal experience about the unwillingness of the community to modify its physical and social environment to enable them to live a better life. As part of this process we label them *the* deaf, or *the* blind, or *the* physically handicapped, but such depersonification does not change the reality of the world—disabled people, neighbours, and 'passers-by', are people. The first step towards the normalizing of a disabled person's environment must be the recognition of his human individuality. The evolution of man's attitudes towards his fellows, disabled or otherwise, is a gradual process, and it often takes many years for change to become observable. Depersonalizing people is a useful technique for avoiding problems, and, indeed, it is a necessary technique for survival. We simply could not cope if all our relationships had to be personal, so we do not attempt to make them so. We identify people (and things) as members of a 'class' and respond on the basis of certain expectations about how members of that class will react and respond to us. We do not expect dogs to talk to us because it is not a characteristic of dogs; similarly, we do not expect people to growl or bark, at least not in the literal sense. When we meet a dog we do not find it necessary to investigate its fluency in speech—we 'know' that it does not talk, just as we know it will have four legs and will eat meat, but will only rarely have blue eyes and eat carrots. The problem of the classification of disabled people is twofold. First, they exhibit some characteristics, such as being a man with one leg, that are different from those we regard as characteristic of 'humans'. Second, they exhibit some characteristics that *seem* to be more characteristic of other classes, such as the poor speech of the deaf person who has been profoundly deaf from birth. It is these seemingly negative attributes that predominate, and disabled people tend, in the mass, to become a class apart—human but less human than ourselves.

We will investigate this problem in more detail later in this chapter, but before doing so it is necessary to establish that disabled people are worthy of interest and concern and to identify the environmental factors that cause disability.

Size of the problem

The problem of disability is not a small one. In the USA the President's Committee on the employment of the handicapped estimated there were over 11 million Americans aged 16 to 64 classifiable as mentally or physically handicapped, 1 in 13 of the population. We do not have strictly comparable figures for Britain, but what evidence we have strongly suggests that this kind of proportion is likely to be found in most advanced industrial countries.

If we include people aged 65 and over the problem assumes even greater numerical significance. There are about $6\frac{1}{2}$ million people aged 65 years and over living in England, representing about 13 per cent of the population. In recent years their numbers have grown by around 100 000 a year, and they will probably continue to do so at the same rate until about 1977/78, before slowing down and stabilizing at round about 7 million by the turn of the century. They represent an increasing proportion of the total population, and more importantly, over the next twenty years the number aged 75 and over is expected to increase by one-third. The number aged 85 and over is expected to increase even more, by 50 per cent. The risk of disability increases sharply with advancing age (see Chapter 6), but the demands and the pressures on the social services are considerable if we allow only for unmet need. They will be added to by the growth and the changing character of the elderly population, and the lack of balance between needs and resources seems likely to continue into the foreseeable future.

The risks to which old people are exposed are symptomatic of the problems of all handicapped and disabled people. We tend to think of them as problems of declining function, but as Figure 1 shows the chief barrier to maintenance of capacity in old people is environmental disease rather than the gradual loss of physical function. Even the most serious decline, in maximum breathing capacity, shows that the average old person, aged 75, retains 43 per cent of the breathing capacity of a young adult. The loss is enough in most cases to impair functioning, but not enough to cause chronic disability. At the other end of the continuum of age, the effects of simple environmental changes such as the level of nutrition in counteracting both the effects of disease and loss of function, are clearly illustrated in Figure 2. The age of the onset of puberty (menarche) parallels the general increase in health standards in the developed countries, where it has consistently declined from an age of 16 to 17 years 120 years ago, to an age of 13 to 14 years in the 1960s.

There is also a growing body of evidence which suggests a possible causative relationship between socio-economic deprivation and poor intellectual capacity. While certain types of severe subnormality tend to be distributed between different social classes in the same way as those

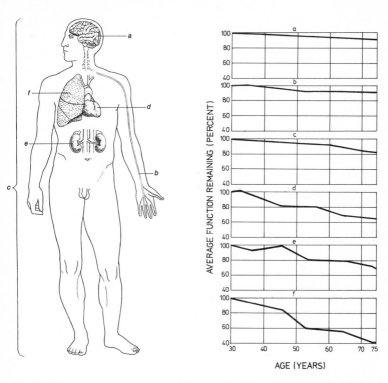

LOSS OF FUNCTION with increasing age does not occur at the same rate in all organs and systems. Graphs (*right*) show loss as a percentage, with the level of function at age 30 representing 100 per cent. Thus brain weight (a) has diminished to 92 per cent of its age-30 value by age 75 and nerve-conduction velocity (b) to about 90 per cent. The basal metabolic rate (c) has diminished to 84 per cent, cardiac output at rest (d) to 70 per cent, filtration rate of the kidneys (e) to 69 per cent and maximum breathing capacity (f) to 43 per cent. Diseases, however, rather than gradual diminution of function, are at present the chief barrier to extended longevity.

FIGURE 1   The decline of different physical capacities as a function of age. (Source: Leaf, A. 1973. Getting old. *Scientific American*, **229**, 3, 52)

classes are distributed in the general population, children classified in Britain as Educationally Subnormal (mild) (ESN (M)) come mainly from the poorest sections of society.

Dobbing and Sands (1973) provided strong evidence of the effects of nutritional deficiencies in mothers and children on subsequent intellectual development; and work ranging from Skeels & Dye (1939) through to that of Clarke & Clarke (1976) has demonstrated that following massive and sustained environmental changes (for example through adoption) many 'subnormal' children from deprived homes or institutions show stable increments in intelligence as measured by standard tests. It is at least a tenable hypothesis that large numbers of

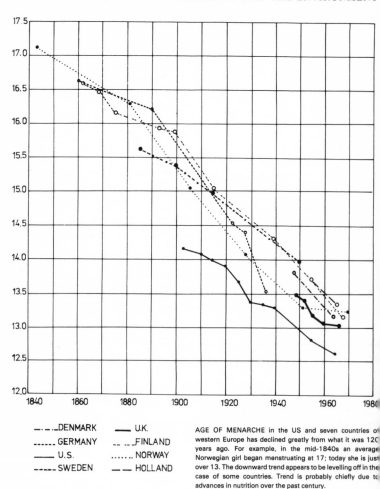

FIGURE 2   The decline in the age of onset of puberty over the last 120 years. (Source: Tanner, J. M. 1973, Growing up. *Scientific American*, **229**, 3, 43)

children currently classified as Educationally Subnormal (mild) might be 'cured' by improvements in social conditions and better educational treatment.

The extent of the problem is indicated in a major study undertaken by the National Children's Bureau (1970). The study defines the disadvantaged child by reference to three environmental factors:

1. the child who lives in a one-parent family, or a family of five or more children;
2. the child who receives free school meals or whose family receives supplementary benefit;
3. the child who lives in accommodation where the density exceeds $1\frac{1}{2}$ persons per room, or where there is no exclusive hot water supply.

One in 16 of the population of Great Britain is disadvantaged by these criteria, and the South of England where only 1 in 47 is so

FIGURE 3 'One-parent family . . . low income . . . poor housing.' (Photograph: Nick Hedges for Shelter)

disadvantaged compares strikingly with the North of England where the ratio is 1 in 12. One in every 20 children living in these conditions was placed in a school for the educationally subnormal whereas the proportion for the total population is 1 in 150.

If it is true that many children do not achieve their full intellectual potential because of the lack of a suitable environment in which to develop, then it is likely that physically disabled children are particularly prone to suffer in this respect because of the tendency to make assumptions about the low level of achievement they can reach. A good example of this was provided when one of the authors was developing, with colleagues, a test of communication skill for use with deaf children. 'Experts' poured scorn on the test, saying, 'Deaf children will *never* do that!' In fact, the research was placed in difficulty because the deaf children, on average, got 70 per cent of the items right, and in consequence discrimination at the upper end of the scale was limited. Zero to 70 per cent in one easy lesson?

Interaction between environment and disability

The importance of environmental effects in disability can be demonstrated in another way when we consider changes in the prevalence of handicapping conditions between childhood and the adult years. Table 2 shows the prevalence of different handicapping conditions in a thousand children, the information being drawn from two different sources: (i) the Seebohm Report on the reorganization of the social services (1968), and (ii) the 'National Child Development Study', the large-scale longitudinal study of the development of children referred to in the previous section. It can be seen from the table that the most frequent causes of mild handicap in children are speech defects, asthma and eczema. In children, the influence of toxic environmental agents is relatively low, although we are not suggesting that such

TABLE 2

The estimated prevalence rate per 1000 children of different handicaps as produced in the Seebohm Report and the National Child Development Study. (Source: Younghusband *et al.* 1970. *Living with Handicap. Report of a Working Party on Children with Special Needs*. Table 2. London: National Children's Bureau)

Handicap	Appendix Q: Seebohm report 5–15-year-olds	National Child Development Study (Cohort 1958) 7-year-olds
Blind and partially sighted	1·2	1·9
Deaf and partially hearing	1·2	1·1
Epileptic	7·2	6·2
Speech defects	27·0*	23·3
Cerebral palsy	3·0	2·2
Heart disease	2·4	3·6
Orthopaedic condition	3·4	4·6
Asthma	23·2	27·4
Eczema	10·4	24·7
Diabetes	1·2	0·2
Other physical handicaps	6·7	6·7
Severely subnormal	3·5	2·7

* 5-year-olds

influences can or should be ignored. In contrast, Table 3 shows that the most prevalent causes of disability in the adult population of Great Britain owe at least as much to environmental toxicity as they do to organic causes. Of course, in many of the conditions affecting adults, the environmental causes are complex and their importance has to be weighed against the importance of other beneficial changes in the environment which may have increased their significance in modern life. Nevertheless, the relationship between pollution and heart and lung

TABLE 3

The main causes of impairment in the adult population of Great Britain. (Source: Harris, A. I., Cox, E. & Smith, C. R. W. 1971. *Handicapped and Impaired in Great Britain*. Part 1, Table A4. London: HMSO. *Reproduced by permission of the Controller of Her Majesty's Stationery Office*)

	Estimated numbers living at home		
	Men and Women	Men	Women
Diseases of bones and organs of movement	1 187 000	351 000	836 000
Diseases of circulatory system	492 000	199 000	292 000
Diseases of central nervous system	360 000	163 000	197 000
Diseases of respiratory system	284 000	179 000	104 000
Disorders of sense organs (including blindness)	277 000	92 000	186 000
Amputations	129 000	105 000	24 000
Senility and ill-defined conditions	122 000	40 000	82 000
Injuries	114 000	73 000	41 000
Mental, psycho-neurotic and personality disorders	98 000	38 000	60 000
Diseases of digestive system	82 000	35 000	47 000
Allergic, endocrine, metabolic and nutritional diseases	51 000	16 000	35 000
Diseases of genito-urinary system	35 000	9 200	26 000
Infective and parasitic diseases	30 000	17 000	12 000
Diseases of blood and blood-forming organs	28 000	4 100	24 000
Neoplasms	27 000	13 000	15 000
Diseases of skin and cellular tissue	20 000	9 400	11 000
Congenital malformations	16 000	5 500	10 000
Totals	3 352 000	1 349 200	2 002 000

conditions is fairly clearly established, and the remedies are mainly determined by economic rather than scientific factors. A different physical environment would significantly reduce the incidence of such disorders.

We could reduce the incidence of injuries and amputations too by better engineering techniques and a change in social values, but to do so might require more significant changes in our life-style than would be acceptable. Lowering speed limits has at least a temporary effect on the incidence of road traffic accidents, but there is probably a level below which speed limits would become self-defeating—flouting the law would become so prevalent that the lower limits would become inoperative. Good design can reduce the incidence of accidents, but many accidents arise from human failure and can only be controlled by a process of public education.

Legislation and disability

Public concern about disability has a long and fascinating history. The earliest reflection of this concern is probably found in Hebraic Law which is the first clearly documented account of an exhortation to help the handicapped. It was an ethic that did much to change the Greek ethos of allowing handicapped children to die in the interests of racial purity. Indeed, it is tragic that the race who espoused this alternative should be subject to persecution and 'extermination' themselves, and that in the twentieth century this should also be undertaken in the interests of 'racial purity'. The incorporation of Hebraic Law into Christianity meant that as early as the fourth and fifth century AD Christian brotherhoods were opening institutions for the blind, and the first such institution in Britain was opened in London in 1329. The first Elizabethan era saw the beginnings of the 'Poor Law' and parish relief from which has developed, with many attitudinal and organizational changes, the present-day social security system and the social service departments of local authorities.

The eighteenth and nineteenth centuries saw a rapid growth in these activities, much of it geared to controlling 'hooliganism' which was feared as a consequence of the industrial revolution. The end result in Great Britain was a greater central government involvement in 'disability', but this concern tended to incorporate disability under the broader umbrella of the 'indigent poor', with certain exceptions. For example, the late nineteenth century saw legislation introduced permitting the provision of special schools for the education of blind and deaf children and the 1899 Education Act extended this permission to schools for physically and mentally handicapped children; and some disability associated with industrial injury has been covered by various Acts, the first being the Workman's Compensation Act of 1897. However, it was not until the 1940s that a special concern about disability began to reveal itself clearly in the 1944 Education Act which *required* all local authorities to provide for pupils who suffered from any disability of mind or body, and in the Disabled Persons (Employment) Act in the same year. But even the National Assistance Act of 1948 was a general measure. It permitted but did not mandate for the development of special services for disabled people. Of course it should not be thought that the disabled have been entirely neglected—the major and often underrated changes in our social fabric in housing, social services, social security, health and education have had major consequences for disabled people, and they have benefited as much as other members of the community. Indeed special provision would be of little value if we did not have a reasonable baseline of general provision as a starting-point. Local authorities have achieved much, thanks to the broad financial support which allows them to cater to the specific and special needs of their local areas. Only employment, vocational training and social security have for historical reasons been centralized. Social security provision is mainly concerned with the problem of income maintenance, and is, therefore, summarized in Chapter 7. The provisions for employment are also better discussed at the relevant points in other parts of the book, except to say that the Employment Services Agency provides a special employment, rehabilitation and placement service for disabled workers.

The pattern of involvement by government agencies in the USA is up to this point similar to that found in Great Britain. Active participation by central agencies has been in social security and employment, although there are marked differences in the way in which that pattern is implemented. Both countries also have a strong tradition of voluntary support, of emphasizing the role of local government as a provider of services, and of legislating disability under the umbrella of more broadly based legislation. Similar concerns exist in most of the developed countries, and as a result supra-national organizations have become involved as well. The European Economic Community (EEC) has an extensive schedule for the development of social welfare programmes, but this is primarily geared to cost benefits and the health services and their harmonization, or to a general perception of the needs of families. The United Nations Educational Social and Cultural Organization (UNESCO) has concentrated on the needs of disabled children, and as well as reports on their educational needs it has made practical assistance and expertise available through its 'aid' programmes.

The break between the common British and American pattern came in 1970 when the Chronically Sick and Disabled Persons Act was passed in Great Britain. This Act is an important watershed not only because of the new legislation introduced. It also served to stimulate public concern for disabled people. The provisions of the 1970 Act are complex, but in broad structure it did three things: it required local authorities to identify and meet some of the needs of disabled people; it gave disabled people a *right* of access to a large number of facilities to which they were denied entry for physical reasons; and although it could not change public attitudes, to some degree it reflected them, and for the first time the *general* needs of disabled people were given public recognition in the most definitive way possible, an Act of Parliament. As a result it is fair to say that disability became a matter of continuing public debate and objective standards were required against which progress can be measured. It did not do everything—no single Act of Parliament could—but a start has been made in an Act that was identified with no particular political ideology or creed.

The causes of disability

We have already referred to many environmental causes of disability. Our purpose here is to provide a structural analysis of these causes, remembering that they are to some degree relative and that the specific causes of disability can and do change from one generation to the next. Indeed, man's evolution has been a constant battle, waging the resources of human ingenuity against the forces of nature. We tend to think of present-day man as the pinnacle of evolution, but of course he is not. He represents the stage of development that evolution has currently reached—who is to say what in the future may be the highest form of life or what in the future may be defined as handicap? A 'hairy' man is handicapped in some respects in the modern world—so much so that most remove unwanted facial hair for cosmetic reasons. It is a hypothetical possibility that one day we may have a similar view of arms, legs, ears and eyes, and if we ever reach the Orwellian state of *1984* there is little question that many so-called 'educationally subnormal' people will be better equipped to survive than most of us who at present define ourselves as 'intelligent'! *Twenty Thousand Leagues under the Sea was* fiction—will the bionic creatures of television turn out to be equally prophetic, and will even they with their collection of electronic spare parts be the ultimate of prosthetic development?

1)   Toxic agents
A great deal of disability is produced by toxic agents including living organisms whose invasion of the human body results in infectious disease. Some of these agents produce easily recognized symptoms as in pneumoconiosis and severe lead poisoning, and those who have seen their effect will have no difficulty in appreciating the damage that they can cause. No less than fifty different diseases are designated 'industrial diseases' for purposes of compensation under the original National Insurance Industrial Injuries Act (1946) or subsequent amendments as incorporated into the Social Security Act (1973) and its

amendments. In addition, sufferers from pneumoconiosis and byssinosis qualify for disablement benefit but not for industrial injuries benefit. Table 4 shows the number of new claims made in the different industries in the specified period. The list of prescribed diseases does not cover all the toxic conditions that can result in industrial disease, but it probably covers the major ones. Other non-industrial conditions, such as a middle ear infection resulting from recurring colds, are usually less obvious and less immediately traumatic, but their long-term effects can be equally disabling. The need for greater control of environmental pollution is, of course, a matter of wide public debate, but the fact that as many as a quarter of a million children in the USA may still be exposed to lead poisoning through lead water-pipes, old paints and similar hazards emphasizes how important this lobby is and how we must ensure that we do not leave a similar legacy for our great-grandchildren.

TABLE 4

New spells of injury benefit paid in respect of the prescribed diseases in the specified industries between 2 June 1975 and 5 June 1976. (Source: Department of Health and Social Security, 1978)

	Poisoning		All Diseases		
Industry	Males	Females	Males	Females	Total
1 Agriculture, Forestry, Fishing	1	0	162	35	197
2 Mining and Quarrying	1	0	1805	4	1809
3 Food, Drink and Tobacco	1	0	351	484	835
4 Chemicals and Allied Industries	8	0	366	105	471
5 Metal Manufacture	9	0	558	79	637
6 Mechanical Engineering	2	0	776	169	945
7 Electrical Engineering	4	0	294	350	644
8 Shipbuilding and Marine Engineering	1	0	133	4	137
9 Vehicle Manufacturing	1	0	457	81	538
10 Textiles	0	0	168	186	354
11 Leather, Leather Goods, Fur and Clothing and Footwear	0	0	126	197	323
12 Bricks, Pottery, Glass, Cement, etc.	1	0	421	130	551
13 Timber, Furniture, etc.	1	0	197	31	228
14 Paper, Printing and Publishing	0	0	166	127	293
15 Construction	3	0	961	14	975
16 Gas, Electricity and Water	0	0	122	4	126
17 Transport and Communication	1	0	283	32	315
18 Distributive Trades	12	0	376	242	618
19 Professional and Scientific Services	0	2	88	337	425
20 Miscellaneous Services such as Hotels	0	0	276	626	902
21 Public Administration and Defence	0	0	144	81	225
22 Other Miscellaneous Industries	14	0	814	462	1276

Control of disease is less easy than control of man-made pollution, at least in the sense that we have some choice in generating the materials that lead to the latter. Nevertheless, the impact of modern medicine has been as much through preventive public health programmes as through the physical or surgical treatment of disease. In the 'advanced' countries adequate sanitation resulting from an understanding of the process of disease transmission, and vaccination and immunization programmes have prevented as much disease as antibiotics have cured or contained, and probably more. Even so there are still vast areas of the earth's surface where preventable and curable disabling conditions such as malaria and leprosy are still endemic (see Table 5).

The difficulty in both the methods of control of disease that we have discussed is that we are rapidly passing the stage where major breakthroughs in engineering or medical research are likely, although there are some areas, such as the common cold, where the breakthrough remains to be made. Control of the environment and public health programmes have now moved into the area of public education, and, unfortunately, man is proving a much more intractable enemy to his own good health than the mosquito larvae or the smallpox virus. Heart disease in the middle years, primarily resulting from poor living habits, is a major 'killer' and a significant 'disabler', but changing people's life-styles is easier said than done.

TABLE 5

Prevalence of and deaths from the specified diseases by different regions. (Source: World Health Organization. 1975. *The World Health Statistics Annual for 1971.* Vol. II. *Infectious Diseases: Cases, Deaths and Vaccinations.* Geneva: World Health Organization)

	Typhoid and Para Typhoid Fever	TB Resp and TB other	Leprosy	Infectious Hepatitis	Typhus and other Rickettsioses	Malaria all cases
a) *Prevalence*						
Africa	22 637	107 155	92 154	43 852	4 082	4 344 749
America	60 641	292 692	9 676	118 642	330	326 976
Asia	50 488	756 437	7 846	32 724	170	296 272
Europe	22 007	437 971	166	308 027	74	5 233
Oceania	241	11 640	5 768	13 275	11	16 463
b) *Deaths*						
Africa	464	4 001	2 569	609	24	4 086
America	2 818	3 293	26	1 014	6	179
Asia	1 390	64 396	620	1 351	4	5 329
Europe	263	39 626	23	2 399	3	34
Oceania	1	471	17	72	—	101

2) Traumatic factors

Another major group of causes of disability is what we choose to term the traumatic. In Great Britain in 1973 there were approximately 7000 deaths from road accidents, 6000 deaths from accidents in the home and 5000 deaths by violence (including self-violence through suicide). On the road there were 89 000 cases of serious injury, and accidents in the home resulted in 90 000 admissions to hospital. On the face of it one might assume that it is safer to drive a car than to stay at home! Any direct comparison of the figures is however invalid, partly because most people spend much more time in their homes than in their cars, and partly, though less obviously, because different reporting procedures obtain for road and home accidents. While the law requires every road accident involving personal injury to be reported to the police, far less stringent procedures are prescribed for the collection of data on accidents in the home. Indeed, safety in the home is still a much neglected area of legislation. Much personal injury might be prevented by greater attention to the design of domestic furniture, tools and equipment, and (with children particularly in mind) the placement of electrical fitments and gas taps. Child-proof tablet containers and medicine bottles are also long overdue. But whether a serious injury occurs at home, at work or on the road, the result for the individual may be a sudden and complete change in his status and life-style. A normal and healthy person becomes, often in the space of a few seconds, one of the 'disabled'.

Some but not all traumatic causes of disability interact either with the toxic causes of disability or with the environmental or social causes we shall discuss in succeeding paragraphs. We can illustrate this interaction in infant mortality using data collected by the European Economic Community (Table 6). It is encouraging to note that all countries in the EEC showed a decline in the number of deaths in the year after birth during the 1960s, and it is generally accepted that much of this decline must be attributed to improved social conditions and health care. Indeed, only factors such as these would explain the change in the relative status of the United Kingdom—since during the period covered there have been no major changes in the causes of infant mortality. From having the second lowest rate in 1960, the UK declined to fifth in the 'league table' in 1973, but the table masks the fact that the problem has been improved in other European countries mainly as a result of a decline in the number of children who die immediately after birth or shortly thereafter. Once this period is past the rates have stayed fairly much the same in the period covered by the table.

The interaction between causes of disability may be illustrated by reference to one type of epilepsy. In some cases epileptic symptoms are the result of trauma, i.e. damage to the brain at birth. These symptoms

TABLE 6

Infant mortality: the number of deaths under the age of one year per 1000 live births in the member countries of the European Economic Community. (Source: European Coal and Steel Community, European Economic Community, European Atomic Energy Commission. 1975. *Report on the Development of the Social Situation in the Community in 1974*. Section D, p. 260. Luxembourg: Office for Official Publications of the European Community)

Year	Belgium	Germany	France	Italy	Luxembourg
1960	31·2	33·8	27·4	43·9	31·5
1965	23·7	23·8	21·9	36·0	24·0
1970	20·5	23·4	18·2	29·2	25·0
1971	19·8	23·1	17·2	28·3	22·5
1972	18·2	22·4	16·0	27·0	14·0
1973	17·0	22·7	15·4	25·7	15·3

Year	Netherlands	United Kingdom	Ireland	Denmark	EUR-6	EUR-9
1960	16·5	22·4	29·3	21·5	33·6	30·8
1965	14·4	19·6	25·3	18·7	26·3	24·6
1970	12·8	18·5	19·2	14·2	22·7	22·0
1971	12·1	17·8	18·0	13·5	21·9	20·8
1972	11·7	17·6	17·7	12·2	20·8	19·9
1973	11·5	17·2	17·8		20·3	

may be only intermittently disabling with long periods when the individual is not visibly different from anybody else. Given early diagnosis and treatment to stabilize the condition and bring the fits under control there is no reason why most epileptics should not live a normal life in the community. Residential treatment may be necessary in more serious cases where the trauma results in additional physical malfunction or personality disorder, although even in these cases the problem is often the lateness of diagnosis and/or the inadequacy of treatment. Unfortunately, despite this objective view of their condition, epileptics are frequently a 'shunned' group. The stigma of epilepsy on a job application form will arouse irrational fears, and make employment in even the mildest case difficult. Apart from the generalized prejudice against disabled people, epileptics still suffer from the attitudes generated over the years that their fits are 'possession by the devil'. Few of us believe this any more, but many of our responses are conditioned by the historical legacy of this belief.

3)   Structural factors

Toxic agents and traumatic factors are environmental causes of disability of a certain type. An equally significant environmental cause of disability is inappropriate ergonomics and design. The motor vehicle causes disability because it is involved in road accidents. It also causes disability because it is not designed to cope with the person who lacks normal physical mobility, and disabled people are not usually part of the mass market to which it is geared. Nevertheless, disabled people are a significant market—about one in twenty people have some form of mild or severe disability which makes it difficult for them to use an urban environment designed for those in normal physical health. Overcoming the problems of the lack of consumer choice will not be easy, although as we said in the first chapter the technology for doing so already exists. It will not be easy because to be truly effective it requires structural planning for the whole environment, not just piecemeal adaptation or planning to deal with a specific type of problem. Kitchen design for wheelchair-users or other types of disabled people is one area where human ingenuity has paid off handsomely, but a kitchen from which escape is impossible can be as much a prison as the Victorian poor-house. It is pleasanter and more efficient, but it is still inadequate. Community planning for the disabled must include housing, transportation, recreation, social services, education, work, hospitals and medical services and shopping facilities. The requirement in the Chronically Sick and Disabled Persons Act (1970) that public buildings, including schools and colleges, must make provision for disabled people, and the display of the well-known symbol indicating such provision, is an important step forward. However, all this is of little use to the disabled person who cannot leave his own home or get into the building in the first place, or to the disabled child who may have access to a school designed to cater for his needs, but is denied admission because there is no teacher trained to teach him.

The design of a suitable environment for disabled people includes more than the ergonomic aspects; it includes for both adults and children the 'learning environment'. It is easy to equate this concept with a classroom, but more learning takes place outside the classroom than inside it. Radio is for most of us a fringe benefit of modern technology, mainly superseded by television. For a blind person it is a vital and crucial link with the world at large—without it he would be cut off from the communication of news and current affairs which most of us take for granted. Deaf people have a similar need for 'captioned' television or television programmes using a visual sign language; both are technically feasible, but at present only limited attempts are made by society to cater for this special need. Education, re-education and vocational training and re-training are crucial areas where much can be done to help disabled people develop new and compensatory skills. Adequate preparation for employment will not enable disabled people to find the right job, but without it there will never be an opportunity for

JOHN JOEY DEACON

Part 1

MAY THE TWENTY-FOURTH NINETEEN TWENTY

OTTINGDON STREET,
WOLLING ROAD,
CAMBER WELL,

This is where my life begins. After I was born, my mother was in bed, my Grandma Brewer heard a knock on the door and when she opened the door, it was my Dad coming home from the army. Grandma Brewer called to her daughter my mother to tell her that her husband had come home from the army.

Part 2

And my mum felldown the stairs before I was born. When I was one year old my mum put me on the kitchen floor, and I used to roll all over the place. Six months after my Dad bought me a chair with table and you could alter it, low or high, and when my mum put my chair low I used to kick the buds out of the garden. Six months after I was two years old.

FIGURE 4 *Tongue Tied*: (a) the original typescript. Each 'part' of four to six lines represents one day's work by the team. (b) *opposite*: the production team. From left to right: Tom, Ernie, Joey and Michael at work. (Source: Deacon, J. J. 1974. *Tongue Tied*. London: National Society for Mentally Handicapped Children)

them to escape from the 'poverty' of disablement. The disabled person needs not only the gadgets—he needs the skill as well. Without the skill he will be unable to obtain maximum, if any, benefit from the gadgets, and it is not surprising that in many cases appliances are discarded as useless. Ergonomics is the offspring of the marriage of experimental psychology and engineering, but at its present state of development it fails to take full account of the aptitude of an individual for learning, and of the degree to which motivation and personality affect the capacity to benefit from a machine. The disabled person is not an

extension of the machine, nor is the machine an extension of him—he is a human personality. He must have as much opportunity to learn by experience and to operate choice as the rest of us, for without such opportunities he will be unable to adapt to his environment and reach his potential.

We can illustrate the problems of the interaction between learning and environment by describing how a recent book (Deacon, 1974) came to be written. Michael could not understand Joey, a spastic resident of a mental hospital, but Michael could 'read and write'. Ernie could after months of patient learning understand Joey's 'spastic' speech, but he could not write. Joey passionately wished to tell his story to the world, but could only tell it to Ernie. So Joey told Ernie, who told it to Michael who wrote it down and Tom typed it out letter by letter because although he could type, he couldn't read. They worked together at a rate of something like two sentences a day. The result: *Tongue Tied*, a moving account of what it is like to be spastic, to be able to understand what is happening yet unable to communicate, and of how opportunity can lead to achievement.

4) Deficiency factors

A fourth way in which the environment can fail the individual is by *not* supplying him with the basic necessities of healthy living, which

include warmth, shelter and an adequate and well-balanced diet. Cold
and exposure can produce general debility and increase susceptibility to
infection. In the very young and the very old hypothermia is a not
infrequent cause of death.

Malnutrition is still the major disabling factor in the poor throughout
the entire third world. It has direct disabling effects. It also decreases the
individual's capacity to resist other disabling conditions. Two forms of
malnutrition are commonly distinguished:

(i)   *Undernutrition*, resulting from getting too little to eat over an
extended period of time. Muscle and fat waste away in the under-
nourished, they become weak and lack energy, and growth in young
children is stunted.

(ii) *Specific nutritional deficiencies*, associated with an inadequate
intake of some particular nutrient (protein, mineral substance or
vitamin). Kwashiorkor is perhaps the best known (because the most
widespread) of the diseases associated with a deficiency or total lack of
protein-calories in early childhood. It demonstrates the difficulty of
assigning disabling conditions to specific environmental causes. While
the principle cause is always malnutrition, genetic, traumatic and
infective factors are almost invariably associated with kwashiorkor.
Also, while it is largely a disease of poverty, culturally determined
practices in childrearing frequently play a part, including changes in
traditional practices on coming into contact with new cultures. The
growing popularity of bottlefeeding in many parts where breastfeeding
has always been the tradition, for example, has resulted in children
being weaned onto inadequate milk or vegetable preparations. The
specific deficiency diseases best known in the western world are rickets,
caused by a deficiency of vitamin D, which can lead to life-long bone
deformities if untreated, and several different types of anaemia each
associated with different specific deficiencies.

The more dramatic disabling effects of undernutrition and specific
deficiencies are fortunately rare today in our own culture. Where they
appear they are not the result of an absolute deficiency in resources but
of faulty distribution. Western agriculture is certainly capable of
producing at least a sufficiency for all, and it has been shown that
young, untutored children, given free access to the ingredients of a well-
balanced diet, will choose for themselves at least enough of all they need
for adequate nutrition. Dietary deficiencies, either at the gross or the
much more common subclinical level, are in our society in the large
majority of cases associated with poverty and, again, those most at risk
are young children in large families and old people with low incomes.

There is a third form of nutritional problem, viz. *overnutrition*, or the pathological results of eating and/or drinking too much. However, the effects are too well known to require further description, except to emphasize that the problem can become pathological as in, say, alcoholism or when food becomes a substitute for affection.

It is, however, ironical that in some countries alcoholism and obesity, with the associated disabling conditions, hypertension and heart disease, are on the increase, while the majority of the human race still subsist on diets which make it unlikely that they will ever know the experience of full health and vigour.

5)   Social agents

The social causes of disability have two interlinked perspectives. First, there is the general decay of some areas, which provide a breeding-ground for toxic and traumatic agents or have a general and diffuse effect on human motivation and achievement. Second, there are the cultural values and individual attitudes towards disability and disabled people. It is these two dimensions of disability that provide the communality lacking in other types of definition, because often when we are discussing disability we classify symptoms to arrive at a diagnosis of a 'disease condition'—we use the medical model described in the first chapter. In contrast, the social model accepts that the environmental effects of different disabilities may be similar and that as a result social remediation may call for general measures. Neither approach is wholly satisfactory, but taken together rather than separately they add to each other and give a more complete picture.

A classic definition of areas of high social need is given in the Home Office circular which launched its Urban Aid programme in 1968: '. . . areas of acute social need are localized districts . . . They are districts which bear the marks of multiple deprivation which may show itself, for example, by way of notable deficiencies in the physical environment, particularly in housing; overcrowding of houses; family sizes above the average; persistent unemployment; a high proportion of children in trouble or in need of care, or a combination of these.' Unfortunately, identifying a need and developing effective administrative mechanisms to meet that need are two different problems. As a result positive discrimination in favour of areas of adverse social conditions is often arbitrary in its effect and fails to reach the 'target population'. Moreover, much of the effort is directed at bricks and mortar, which does nothing to meet social needs and sometimes generates new ones. For example, we are now beginning to realize that the idealistic replacement of slums by dehumanized tower blocks of flats destroys social networks and inhibits the development of new ones. Particularly for young mothers and the old and disabled it results in isolation and loneliness, which in turn results in depression, itself a disabling condition.

The effects of environment on educational, psychological and social attainments have also been further confused by the tendency to presuppose that a good environment is defined as a good middle-class environment. This problem has plagued the education of black children in inner-city areas of the USA, where the arguments often crystallize around the language of such children, and around the appropriateness or inappropriateness of clinical practice and teaching based on language defined by the prevailing culture. The traditional view of the language of American blacks was that it is a direct descendant of the English used in the southern States (Williamson, 1971). More recently, it is thought to have developed from a number of West African languages, such as Hausa, Wolof, Twi and Mende, which have been modified by exposure to a number of European languages, particularly the original and American form of Portuguese, Dutch, French and English (Dillard, 1972). Taylor (1973) points out that classifying a pronunciation of 'toofbrush' or a statement 'He from Chicago', as abnormal often fails to consider their accuracy as a dialectical pronunciation or an application of a set of language rules different from those used by the prevailing culture. It can lead to the conclusion that children or adults have 'poor language' whereas if a more appropriate set of rules for pronunciation and grammar were used we would find out that there is no difficulty. The problem is not as serious in Great Britain as in the USA, but there is an undoubted need for greater awareness, since it will grow as immigrant cultures become more widely established in our society. Such children are already more frequently placed in special schools, and we must consider how much this is the result of a cultural imbalance.

Attitudes to disability

There are no generalized public attitudes to disabled people of all types, but usually the nearer the disability is to 'sickness', the more positive the attitude. Blind and physically handicapped people are regarded more favourably than deaf or mentally handicapped people, and are more likely to be thought of in terms of the 'good' values we ascribe to handicapped people such as patience, tolerance and even intelligence. Unfortunately, people's behaviour in the mass is not necessarily a reflection of their individual attitudes, as is clearly indicated by the atrocities which are committed in times of severe stress such as war. Few of us are murderers, but with a uniform, a rifle and a social acceptance of what we are doing we can set on one side our individual values and kill in the common cause, though not, of course, even when that cause is admirable in its own right, without considerable conflict for the individual because of the imbalance between his behaviour and his objectives. Similarly, although we may declare our lack of prejudice towards handicapped people, how we behave when we have to meet them as fellow students, workmates and neighbours may be quite different. Even more important is the degree to which our positive feelings dissipate when we are removed from direct contact with disabled people. A television programme about injustice and prejudice will generate social concern, but the effects will be rapidly lost because there will be little follow-up or evaluation of the changes, if any, brought about as a result of this concern. Hopefully, the concerns we will discuss in subsequent chapters will not prove to be quite so ephemeral!

3

Early Childhood and the Family

Sensory development

The traditional perception of disability has been one of abnormality. It is a perception that owes much to the 'medical model' referred to in Chapter 1, whether practised in medicine, psychology or education. It takes as its starting-point the idea of a standard, known as a 'norm', and when a symptom or a condition departs from this norm it is classified as abnormal. A good example is 'body temperature' which is maintained by homeostatic mechanisms so that it is surprisingly constant within very narrow limits. Small variations within these limits have little importance, but once the temperature becomes excessively high or low it indicates that the homeostatic mechanisms have become disturbed or are unable to cope. Coupled with an assessment of other symptoms this can lead to a diagnosis, and through diagnosis to treatment. Psychologists and teachers have often adopted a similar perspective—intelligence or speech of a certain type is 'normal'; there is a range of normal variations but once this range is exceeded we are dealing with something defined as 'abnormality'. There is growing recognition among both research workers and practitioners that this model is inappropriate in the field of disability, particularly where children are concerned. A child, disabled or otherwise, must always be viewed primarily as a developing organism.

The rate at which the child develops and the course of the development vary, but such differences are not abnormalities. Therefore, the concept of a 'norm' has little meaning and only limited value in assessing the psychological and social attributes of disabled children or adults. For this reason this chapter and succeeding ones will look at disability as a continuum of development, in which skills are learned or lost in a logical and progressive sequence. However, since we know little of how the handicapped child and adult develop, we will use knowledge of the development of unimpaired individuals as a framework in which to structure our thinking. This is not to use the unimpaired as the norm; it is simply, whenever useful, to use what is known of the way they function as a basis for comparison. In so doing we emphasize the normality of disability, and a good example is the development of mobility in a physically impaired child confined to a wheelchair. There is no way we can restore mobility to the child's legs, but there are many ways that he can *learn* to use physical aids such as the wheelchair itself to become more mobile, and ways that he can use other parts of the body to achieve the same objective. However, the achieving of this objective will depend crucially on motivation, a motivation that will be encouraged by parents, teachers, doctors and occupational therapists who accept that he is not abnormal, and that given the right opportunities and experiences he can develop normally in his own way.

Within the context just described, the next sections of this chapter will look at the development of physical and cognitive skills in all infants, handicapped or otherwise, for this is the frame in which with rare exceptions the handicapped child will develop. How far he has developed and how far he will, and in which respects he will develop least and most successfully are another matter determined by the nature of his handicap and the environmental support he receives. The later sections of the chapter and much of the following chapter will explore the type of environmental support needed in more detail, but knowing 'how' without knowing 'why' is the problem of much of the help already provided for handicapped children. We cannot fully explain the why, but it is important that we make some attempt to do so if we are to avoid providing only psychological props for the person who supports the child rather than meaningful objectives for his development.

The sensory receptors of the unimpaired infant are all fairly well developed at birth, including the senses of touch, taste and smell, as well as sight and hearing. Very young babies will produce gross reflex responses to stimuli in all these modalities, but decoding the complex patterns of stimulation into a meaningful representation of the environment to which the child can respond selectively involves a long process of learning. In this process each of the senses plays a different particular role, but the total experience is far greater than the sum of the parts, as anyone who has watched an average nine-month-old baby exploring his environment in play will understand. Any small object, say a discarded toffee-wrapping, will be tasted, handled and squeezed, stared at with intense concentration as it changes shape in the hand, and crumpled and crackled near to the ear. Losing it and finding it again are particularly exciting as the concept of its continued existence in time, independent of the presence of an observer, is gradually achieved. The child with a sensory defect, particularly in one of the two most important senses for human development, sight and hearing, is at a major disadvantage at this early, information-gathering stage. He must struggle to make his unimpaired senses perform not only their own jobs, but those of the defective organ as well. Similarly the child with a motor defect is hampered in perceptual learning, if he cannot move adequately in the environment or manipulate objects for examination. It is sometimes suggested that the child who has 'only' a sensory or a motor impairment should be able to compensate by becoming a good scholar. Any disability, however, which impedes basic learning processes also and inevitably puts the child at an intellectual disadvantage at all stages of learning.

Within three years of birth the average child has developed all the basic mechanisms of speech and language, which we shall discuss in the next section. Thereafter, growth is concerned more with refining and developing physical, social and cognitive skills than with the development of basic perceptual processes. Such growth has as its starting-point the sensory receptors of the eyes and the ears, but, as we have already said, impairment of these receptors is not a simple matter of being unable to see or to hear, or to respond to physical stimuli separated physically from the infant. Figure 5 shows how a physical

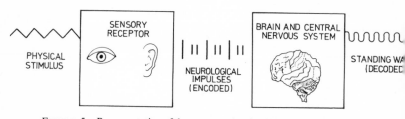

FIGURE 5   Representation of the processes involved in receiving sensory stimuli

stimulus, consisting of trains of waves or impulses, first arrives at a sensory receptor, the eye or the ear. These waves or impulses are encoded into neurological messages which are transmitted to the central nervous system and the brain. The brain decodes the neurological impulses into patterns representative of the original waves or impulses and assigns meaning to them. Thus the process of seeing a table involves three main parts—light reflected from the table forms an image of the table on the retina of the eye, this image is encoded into neural messages transmitted by the optic nerve to the brain, which decodes these messages and identifies the object being viewed as a table. Just as a car can have a breakdown in the wheels, the axle or the engine, the sensory system can have a breakdown in the processes of sensory reception, the processes of 'encoding', or the processes of 'decoding'. Figure 6 illustrates this effect and the nature of the breakdown. Only in the case of damage to the sensory receptors themselves is the process strictly analogous to covering one's eyes or ears and shutting out light and sound. In the other instances, we are dealing with the much more complex problems of coding and interpreting messages. In such cases simply to remove a sensory blockage, as can be done partly with

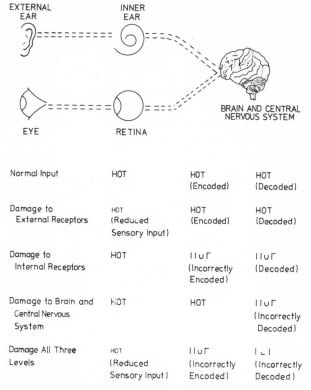

Normal Input	HOT	HOT (Encoded)	HOT (Decoded)
Damage to External Receptors	HOT (Reduced Sensory Input)	HOT (Encoded)	HOT (Decoded)
Damage to Internal Receptors	HOT	IIuΓ (Incorrectly Encoded)	IIuΓ (Decoded)
Damage to Brain and Central Nervous System	HOT	HOT	IIuΓ (Incorrectly Decoded)
Damage All Three Levels	HOT (Reduced Sensory Input)	IIuΓ (Incorrectly Encoded)	IᴗI (Incorrectly Decoded)

FIGURE 6   Representation of the effects of impairment of different parts of the system receiving sensory inputs

spectacles or to a lesser extent with a hearing-aid, is of little if any help in overcoming the effect of the handicap.

Language development

The unimpaired new-born infant gives gross reflex responses only inconsistently, to very loud sounds. These reflexes form the 'startle reflex', but by the age of approximately eight months they will have been modified so that localization of fairly quiet everyday sounds is possible. (It is important to keep in mind, however, that in this respect, and in all generalizations about 'normal' development, there are wide individual variations in the ages at which particular behaviour patterns first appear.) In addition to localizing such sounds the child of this age will also respond by, for example, smiling to very familiar stimuli such as the voice or smile of his mother. Progress is rapid and by the baby's first birthday he will respond to the names of some visually familiar objects or respond to scolding by frowning. Within this complex pattern of behaviour he appears to have developed discrimination for sound in addition to the ability to localize it. The next change concerns the distance at which sounds can be responded to, and by the age of approximately eighteen months the baby will have progressed from responding to sounds at a conversational level only when they are immediately adjacent to him, to responding to such sounds at a distance of several feet or yards provided they are a part of his immediate topological environment. He will also have learned a great deal more about the shapes and sizes of objects as he begins to move around among them and become familiar with the changing patterns they make on the retina of his eye. Additionally, the child will have developed a simple naming vocabulary and will identify the words for some of the major body parts.

The accelerating curve of development continues and at approximately twenty-four months responses to simple verbal commands involving two distinct actions will be obtained and the child will be able to associate a large number of familiar nouns with their referents. At the venerable age of thirty-six months the basis of language will have been developed and the child will be able to understand basic but complex sentence structures involving nouns, verbs, adjectives, prepositions and pronouns. Further development will consist of refining the child's ability to cope with the language that he receives so that more complex sentence structures are perceived correctly and the total amount of cognitive information with which the child can cope is increased.

For simplicity of presentation the previous paragraph discussed the child's ability to perceive sounds and the response that these were capable of producing. The child also makes sounds, but it is important to remember that the sounds he hears and the sounds he makes do not exist in isolation. Each is dependent on the other and abnormal development in one will give rise to abnormal development in the other. The child begins, at birth, by making purely emotive sounds, such as crying when hungry or when he has soiled himself. By eight months he will be making spontaneous vocalizations but these will be undirected and unrelated to the external environment. Gradually, the external environment will achieve some degree of reality at which stage, approximately twelve months, he will start to vocalize in play activities and will try to imitate simple words. Vocabulary will grow through the age of eighteen months until the child at twenty-four months will spontaneously use nouns to identify familiar objects and will learn the names of unfamiliar objects in one or a limited number of presentations.

As with the changes in the receptive vocabulary, the basis of language will have been laid by the age of thirty-six months and the child will usually use simple sentences of three, four, five or six words and have *some* concept of the use of nouns, verbs, adjectives, pronouns and prepositions.

Almost invariably the ability to understand precedes the ability to create, and whilst the two are intimately related and highly correlated, the child will be able to receive much more complex language than he can transmit. He will often recognize words that he cannot use so that, for example, he could recognize the word 'Mummy' at twelve months of age but may not say it until eighteen to twenty-four months of age. Similarly, at thirty months of age he may respond correctly to the command, 'Go into the garage and get the train', but would only issue the command, 'Get train'. This is partly because the formalities of language are redundant, and we do not need to correctly perceive and understand every word and nuance to grasp its meaning. Nevertheless, it also illustrates another important principle—speech can only develop out of appropriately internalized language.

Physical development

One of the earliest manifestations of the interaction between maturation and environment is found in studies of physical development in young infants. Research has shown that physical maturation is important even in behaviour popularly assumed to be primarily socially motivated. The age at which a baby smiles is related to age of conception rather than date of birth, and in consequence babies born prematurely or late still smile at about forty-six weeks after conception, not about six weeks after birth. Environment is important, but it will not begin to operate until a given level of maturity is reached, and a young child may be handicapped in either one or both aspects—he may not have reached the required level of maturation to perform a particular action, as may be the case with, say, a spastic child, or he may not have been able to manipulate his environment successfully, as in the case of a blind child. The difference is important, but somewhat arbitrary. We can only evaluate the maturity of a child by observing how he manipulates the environment, but we should avoid persisting in manipulation of the environment when lack of maturity prevents successful learning. A good example is toilet training. Even in normal children toilet training before the age of about two years will not produce complete control of urine and faeces because the child lacks the necessary motor control, and if one of a pair of twins is trained and the other is not they still achieve full control at about the same age (McGraw, 1940). Many handicapped children are late in becoming toilet trained because parents and teachers do not provide them with the right experiences, but in some cases they are physically immature and, therefore, no amount of training will produce success. It is of course not enough for a doctor to tell parents 'the child will grow out of it'. He needs to make them aware to the best of his knowledge of the limits set by the child's level of physical maturity.

If a given activity is beyond the child we must approach the problem by changing the environment not by asking him to cope when he cannot. We should also be wary of writing children off too quickly, and equating the effects of an impairment on a mature adult with similar effects on a plastic and developing child. Bower (1974) gives a good example, that of a child with congenital arhinencephaly. In this condition the two hemispheres of the brain fail to divide, causing the child to experience continuous random seizures, and a similar phenomenon prevents adults from registering external events in their environment. Nevertheless, Bower reports a child with this condition who did develop the earliest stages of physical development—raising her head in a prone position, supporting herself on her elbows and making co-ordinated movements. We still have much to learn about how children learn to cope with malfunctioning systems.

Our lack of knowledge and the need for appropriate treatment are well illustrated by cerebral palsy. This is the largest single cause of serious physical disability in children and results primarily in spasticity, rigidity of movement and inability to relax the muscles, although athetosis (frequent involuntary body movements) and ataxia (poor balance and a typical unsteady straddled gait) are sometimes present. About three children in a thousand suffer from cerebral palsy, although the rate in the over-forties falls to about one per thousand (Rutter *et al.*, 1970). The disability is a good one to illustrate the need for environmental training and adaptation for the disabled child, and despite their often severe motor problems many spastic children grow up to achieve a high level of independence. If he is to do so it is essential that from as early an age as possible physiotherapists, with support from parents, try to help the spastic child follow as normal a sequence of human development as he can, and that at a later, but not much later, age occupational therapists work with the child to modify the environment to his or her advantage. Children who cannot walk can sometimes ride tricycles with great skill and occasionally excessive enthusiasm, and spastic children whose tremor prevents them using a pencil can often learn to use a typewriter. The limits are set more by human ingenuity and resources than the capacity of the child— complex control systems now exist which can be used by a person completely paralysed except for minimal finger movement.

In the past the handicapped child was treated as a set of distinct skills,

FIGURE 7 A small boy with spina bifida riding a battery-operated toy car adapted from foot control to finger control to encourage mobility. (Photograph: Neville Chadwick—Leicester Red Cross Toy Library for Handicapped Children)

and various professionals remediated those skills for which they were responsible. The physiotherapist dealt with motility and mobility, the speech therapist with speech, the teacher with academic subjects, and the parent with social training. Apart from the problems of a lack of co-ordination and integration in training this also created the problem of what to do with a child during the often long periods of the day when nobody was assigned to work with him as opposed to supervising him.

As a reaction against both problems, many professionals now favour a unified approach to treatment—each retains his special skills, but groups of professionals work with individuals or with groups of children to attempt to set up a total integration with the environment. An extreme example of this is the Peto method, as used with severely cerebral-palsied children in Budapest. Esther Colton and Margaret Parnell (1967) have reported the method in detail, but briefly it involves groups of ten to twenty children living, eating and sleeping with their 'teachers' during a highly structured programme of motor and speech training. The training is designed to fit the child to cope with the rigours of an environment that does not cater specifically for their problems. We must be careful that such systems are not allowed to override the needs of others, particularly parents, but there can be little doubt that the right kind of intensive and integrated effort is the most effective way of manipulating the environment to allow the child to achieve his maximum potential.

Cognitive development

Cognitive development in children may be divided usefully into the classical phases identified by Piaget and his co-workers (e.g. Inhelder and Piaget, 1958). The phases are the Sensory-Motor (ages approximately 0 to 2 years), the Pre-Operational (ages approximately 2 to 7 years), the Concrete Operational (ages approximately 7 to 11 years) and the Formal Operational (ages approximately 11 to 15 years). We can illustrate them by referring to a classic Piagetian experiment in which an unimpaired child is presented with two pieces of plasticine of equal weight and volume rolled into pancake shapes. One of the pieces of plasticine is then rolled into a long sausage. In the pre-operational stage the child responds to the change by indicating that the volume and weight of the 'sausage shape' are greater. At about 7 years of age he says only weight has changed but at about 9 years of age he reverses his position and says only volume has changed. It is not until approximately age 11 that he is able to perceive the principle of conservation of weight and volume and not until the age of approximately 14 years is he able to express this as a formal, logical operation.

The thinking processes discussed by Piaget are normally mediated through language—although it must be remembered that language should not be confused with speech—and the degree to which children develop general social and cognitive skills will depend upon their exposure to language. However, it is also true to say that conventional language is not the only mediator through which the thinking processes can be activated. To understand these apparently contradictory points of view it is useful to refer to the work of Chomsky (*see* Chomsky & Chomsky, 1965). In a complex theory Chomsky postulates the existence of a language acquisition device centred in the brain. This is not a repository of language but it contains the deep structure of language—that is, a set of universal rules which will ultimately determine the syntax of language. Therefore, the child has a pre-existing natural tendency to assimilate and utilize language. In turn, this natural language capacity means that environment is important only in providing 'knowledge of results' and modifying language patterns; not in motivating the child to use language in a form determined by external influences. The initial formulation of the structure of language is done by the child who then modifies this on the basis of feedback from the environment which confirms or disproves the hypothesis he has formulated to explain the world about him. The process explains the propensity of children to ask 'Why?' and to formulate phrases such as 'I goed to town' or 'I goned to town' instead of the grammatically correct form—'I went to town' (Craig, 1968).

The existence of an internal propensity to acquire language explains why not all learning and cognitive process is dependent upon the *formal expressive* language that most of us use in a seemingly natural way. The rules of language are mainly logical ones and, therefore, can be applied in other ways than through a language mediator. Of course, it is difficult to conceptualize 'thinking without language' because most of *our* thinking tends to be with language. However, Furth (1966) has shown fairly conclusively that operations of the sensory-motor, pre-operational and concrete operational type can be performed by deaf children who could not be expected to do so in terms of their knowledge of the formal expressive language of the hearing culture. He states (Furth, 1966):

> We cannot help but express our deep concern that the intellectual growth of the deaf child is so often placed second to his linguistic achievement. We say this not because we underestimate the importance of language. But here, as probably in education in general, it may be a question of understanding or misunderstanding biological priorities. As Piaget points out, in the hearing child the acquisition of linguistic competence is a normal by-product of intellectual growth and language is just one of the many other contemporaneous forms of symbolic behavior in the child. If we must teach language in a formal manner—in itself a rather boring and intellectually not stimulating topic—the present findings suggest that many more things than we ever

thought can be communicated with a minimum of words and
that unused thinking structures of deaf and hearing students
are ready to assimilate the intellectual nourishment which the
structures require.

Unfortunately, Furth omits the consideration of language as a source
of high-level conceptual thinking and orectic (emotional/social)
development. There is an important principle intrinsic to his arguments
and one that is forgotten by many teachers. Furth does, however, over-
generalize in his concern to counteract the repetitive teaching of speech
as if it were language and the continual underestimation of the cognitive
abilities of deaf children. Such concern is understandable, but the failure
to significantly delineate between concrete and abstract thinking and
linguistic and emotional development through language tends to reduce
the effectiveness and the acceptability of his argument. For example,
whilst failure could result from other causes, the slow growth of reading
ability in deaf children from 11 years of age to 16 years of age could
reflect the failure to make the transition to formal operations (see
Wrightstone, Aronow and Moskowitz, 1963). There is a similar delay in
the social development of such children, as crudely measured by a test
known as the Vineland Social Maturity Scale, which only increases by
about 10 per cent between the ages of 15 years and 19–21 years (see
Myklebust, 1964). Therefore, we cannot regard language merely as 'one
of many contemporaneous forms of symbolic behavior in the child', but
as a cornerstone of cognitive and emotional/social development
without which attainments in these areas will *eventually* be limited.

The need of the child to modify his environment and to respond and
be responded to by social language enables us to appreciate that we use
language to control our environment and that socially acceptable
responses will be rewarded whereas socially unacceptable responses
will not. The rewarding of the responses will begin by being physical,
such as the arrival of the mother when called, but will later include
verbal responses such as 'good boy' or the more sophisticated
variations of intonations such as are used with adolescents and adults.
Most handicapped infants probably have a suitable internal mechanism
for handling some kind of language syntax, but a lack of reinforcement
for the use of language and of feedback prevents its development and
ultimately, without remedial help, destroys their motivation to
communicate. Provide them with secondary rewards such as pleasure
and affection from their mother or provide them with primary rewards
such as communication that produces feedback, and the development
of language and communication will become possible, even though in
some cases the form it takes will be different from that used by the
majority.

Practical implications

The development of perceptual, physical, cognitive and linguistic skills in early childhood is crucial, and the experiences the child has in the pre-school years will do much to determine his progress when he enters primary school. One of the better programmes in this field has been developed by Reynell (1973). In summary the programme emphasizes: (i) the use of graded symbolic play material, from large dolls and tea-sets to small model-village play, and two-dimensional picture material; (ii) symbolic gesture is freely used in addition to speech; (iii) direct teaching of verbal comprehension is carried out individually and in small groups; (iv) adults modify their sentence length and vocabulary to each child's level of comprehension; (v) the language used always has a direct and perceptually evident concrete reference, to reinforce the language-meaning link; and (vi) corrective feedback is supplied so that each child can hear correctly what he has attempted to say.

Less formalized approaches have also been used. For example, with educationally subnormal children and adults the use of the manual sign language of deaf people has been found to both motivate and facilitate the development of both language and communication (Walker, 1976). Work such as this confirms what we said earlier—the development of language and speech requires a language system appropriate to the child with whom we are working. Adult spoken speech, even when simplified, had too complex a structure for the severely subnormal patients; as a result the Makaton Vocabulary of signs for the deaf was employed. Once exposed to it, they not only developed simple language and communication, but *speech improved at the same time*. The most important function of the Makaton Vocabulary was to enable staff working with patients to relate to them in an environment that was adapted to their needs, and not to those of the adults who had to care for them.

Environmental experience is of necessity limited for handicapped children, whether by lack of input or lack of opportunity to explore. Consequently, much emphasis has been placed on remedial work in the pre-school or the home designed to replace the missing components of the child's experience. However, the rationale for many of these programmes is a direct or indirect assumption that there are certain 'critical periods' in the development of the child, and failure to facilitate development during these periods will result in a permanent loss of ability. The idea is borrowed from animal psychology and ethology. It is certainly true that early workers in these fields held that 'learning' had to take place during the 'critical periods', and that if it did not or if inappropriate learning took place subsequent change was impossible. More recent research has qualified this hypothesis. It is now generally accepted that the critical periods are not so critical as was once believed, and even if they are, subsequent relearning is possible in a later phase of development (see Clarke & Clarke, 1976). If we are looking at early education from the point of view of *learning*, its main importance is in that the earlier we are able to start work with the child the less likely it is that he will have learned inappropriate ways of responding and the more time he will have to learn more appropriate ways of responding. The teacher is able to concentrate more of her effort into new learning, rather than into remediating earlier inappropriately learned behaviour. On the other hand, it is also true that the child will learn only those things that he or she is developmentally ready to learn, and the earlier sections of this chapter are important because they illustrate the developmental phases through which the child goes, the approximate age at which these phases occur, and the kind of environmental modification necessary if learning is to take place.

The child in the family

To achieve maximum value from working with a child during the pre-school years education should concentrate not only on the achievements of the child but also on the achievements of the family. This point is often forgotten, and even when the programmes directly involve working with the pre-schooler's family, success is often measured by the change in the child's basic physical, perceptual, linguistic, social and/or cognitive skills rather than in the structural relationships and attitudes of the family. The family as part of the child's environment will be discussed in more detail later, but when a handicapped child is born into a family the initial response to this traumatic experience is often a refusal to accept that the child is handicapped. Parents, brothers and sisters, grandparents, aunts and uncles are unrealistic in their evaluation of the child and fail to provide him with adequate emotional support (Broomfield, 1967).

Practitioners of pre-school education often argue that their programmes are designed to meet the needs of the family (e.g. Northcott, 1971), and certainly there are a few programmes that effectively develop an integrated family as the basis for future educational or social development. Unfortunately, such programmes are rare. Education rather than psychology and social work has been the main discipline sponsoring pre-school programmes, and the training and philosophy of most educators is incompatible with the training and philosophy required for family counselling. The training and attitudes of teachers emphasize child-centred achievement, those of psychology and social work emphasize people-centred adjustment. Neither approach is wrong, but both can be and frequently are wrongly applied.

In most cultures the basic unit of socialization is the family and most cultures have some form of structural organization based on the family. A 'nuclear' family structure is particularly typical of North American and English society (see Figure 8), though there is no particular merit in such a structure—it is only one of several possibilities.

One of the most useful differentiations between different parental roles was made some time ago by Parsons and Bales (1955), and like many good ideas it has stood the test of time. Parsons and Bales distinguish between instrumental or expressive parental roles.

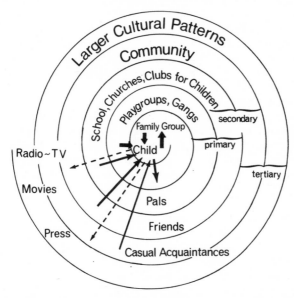

FIGURE 8   Diagram illustrating the way the child's experience widens with age and becomes more dependent on the community and the larger cultural patterns. (Source: Thorpe, Louis P. 1962. *Child Psychology and Development*. 3rd edn. New York: Ronald Press)

Instrumental roles are concerned with exercising control over the child, and to some degree represent an authoritarian approach to child-rearing. Expressive roles are concerned with the emotional aspects of the parenting and in them control is mediated through affection. Meadow and Meadow (1971) have discussed the nature of role perceptions of parents of handicapped children and of the process whereby the parent of a handicapped child is socialized into an appropriate role. They give as examples of instrumental aspects of the role of parents of handicapped children the learning of ways to help cerebral-palsied children to use their muscles or learning to help deaf children use and manipulate their hearing-aids. Examples they give of the expressive aspects of the parental role for a parent of a handicapped child include learning how to cope with the feelings of guilt, shame, or sorrow which naturally follow the parents' discovery that their child is handicapped, and learning to cope with the pity, rejection and avoidance of neighbours and friends. Parents of handicapped children have to learn to cope with both the instrumental and the expressive aspects of their roles if they are to contribute to the overall development of their children. Factors that affect the parents' ability to participate effectively in this socialization process include socio-economic status, age of parents, sex of child, birth order of child, religious orientation and parents' own status as a handicapped or non-handicapped person.

The handicapped child needs a normal family environment to at least as great if not a greater extent than the unimpaired child. Unfortunately, the effect of the handicapped child on the family is to generate within the parents a complex set of responses which can often lead to the development of an abnormal environment. Denial, over-protection, guilt and rejection are characteristic and important parental responses to the handicapped child. Many parents when first told of their child's problems tend to deny the existence of the handicap, and will search for a doctor or teacher who will assure them that their child is 'normal'. Many others respond by over-protecting the child and making him far more dependent than he needs to be. Others blame themselves, and because of their guilt feelings find it difficult to relate to the child. Finally, some parents will reject the child to the extent that a rare few will actually maltreat or abandon him. Indeed this last response has been socially institutionalized in some cultures—the Romans dealt with the problem of deafness by throwing deaf children in the Tiber to drown. Schaefer (1965) has undertaken useful work in quantifying these responses into polar dimensions and the results of his work are summarized in Figure 9, which is self-explanatory.

Some families are capable of resolving the problems just described themselves, but most can benefit from formal or informal counselling designed to change the family environment. Whether from their own resources or with the help of others the resolution of the problems usually passes through five basic stages. The first stage is characterized by a growing awareness that a serious problem exists. This leads to a

FIGURE 9   The three-dimensional framework of parental attitudes to handicapped children developed by Schaefer. The two flat diagrams above can be merged into a three-dimensional structure with circumferences forming the surface of a sphere. The attitudes marked around the edges of the quadrants have been determined by research. (Source: Schaefer, Earl S. 1965. A configurational analysis of children's reports of parent behaviour. In *Contemporary Issues in Developmental Psychology*, ed. N. S. Endler. New York: Holt, Rinehart & Winston)

a) Acceptance v Rejection/ Autonomy v Control

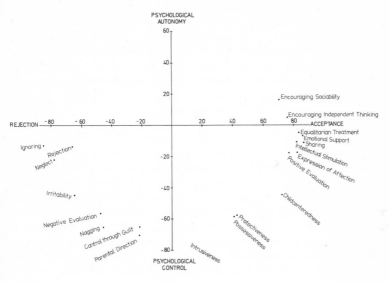

b) Autonomy v Control/ Firm v Lax Control

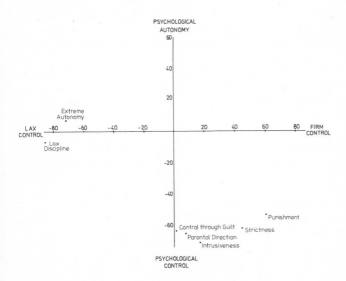

FIGURE 9

recognition of the problem in the second stage, and in the third stage a search for the reason. The fourth stage involves a search for a solution and the fifth and final stage involves acceptance and adjustment to the problems generated by having a handicapped child. The time-span for these progressive responses is variable. It may be collapsed into a period of a few weeks or it may be extended over a period of many years. Indeed, some families fail to reach the final stage, although most eventually do come to accept their handicapped child. However, even families who are well adjusted will find complete acceptance difficult and will intermittently pass through periods of searching for solutions and attempting to assign causes even of a supernatural type. The family environment will always be less than optimal until the handicapped child is completely accepted, although this does not necessarily mean accepting the social consequences of handicap. Nevertheless, it must also be emphasized that parents of handicapped children are no more perfect than parents of normal children. To worry over our mistakes rather than to use them as a basis of learning from experience is a common reaction, but rather short-sighted, and not something to be encouraged. Good examples are 'homework' and the need of all teenagers to spend time on their own daydreaming in a fantasy world. On innumerable occasions parents have approached the authors describing these as problems not of their own child, but of, say, their *deaf* child. Many are surprised when told that if these are 'problems' then everybody has them—few teenagers like homework and all daydream. Because the child is disabled, it is very easy to assume that he behaves the way he does because he is disabled, whereas in fact he would be an atypical child if he did not behave in this way.

The emphasis placed by professionals on *the treatment*, whether of the child or the family, is one factor that increases the stress on the family with a handicapped child. It has been summarized by Townsend and Jaehnig in their study of the families of mentally handicapped children (Jaehnig, 1974):

> Some professional workers in contact with the families lack the expertise to provide them with practical assistance. Others, meant to act as co-ordinators in introducing potential forms of assistance, fail even to make contact with families. The present structure of social services is heavily biased toward residential care and tends therefore to encourage parents to admit their child. Parents of the more severely handicapped find these pressures very strong because of the tendency of services to care for more able children and adults.
>
>   This is due in part to the pervasive influence that professional bodies had in the past on social policy for the

mentally handicapped. No systematic attempt has been made to consider either the domiciliary needs of parents or to consider their preferences in the development of services. When viewed from an external standpoint—divorced from the professional groups or even the parents themselves—the total ineffectiveness of present provision is evidenced in its failure to compensate families for the deprivation they experience. 'Community care', as described by the Royal Commission in 1957, will not become reality until families are fully supported in caring for their handicapped members and the choice of using residential facilities becomes their own.

The unfortunate aspect of these findings is that the use of self-expression for diagnostic and therapeutic purposes has long been realized to be an important principle in work with emotionally disturbed persons. Easson (1969) states: 'In the optimum treatment environment where the patient is allowed reasonable self-expression, he then has to face what kind of self he is expressing and how this measures up against the reality of society's needs and of his own expectations.' The need for such self-expression is as important for the family and the wider society as it is for the individual and for exactly the same reasons—the family or the group needs to identify the image it presents and how this measures up to the needs of society and its collective expectations. A situation of conflict and prejudice will intensify the need for a collective group identity and, therefore, in view of the prejudice towards handicapped children and their parents it is not surprising that the families of handicapped children or certain groups of handicapped adults feel the need to belong to special groups, clubs and organizations. Such groups provide visibility, mutual support and the opportunity to relate to other people in a non-threatening situation.

Families and stress

Personal and family adjustment depends critically on environmental stress, even though genetic and other factors may predispose some of us to be less tolerant of stress or to develop stress reactions of a certain type. A good example of this is the case of twins adopted and raised independently of each other: their adjustment is characteristically more similar to that of their adoptive families than it is to that of their natural families. The presence of a handicapped child in the family is for reasons we have already outlined a focus for environmental stress. Therefore it is not surprising to find that over and above the kinds of reactions that we have described, families of handicapped children are likely to respond inappropriately to other environmental stresses both as a family unit and as individuals within a family unit. Environmental stress of this type is the main causal factor in what has been referred to as the 'cycle of deprivation'. The stresses and strains of one generation result in the development of similar stresses and strains in the third generation. So the problem child *may* become the problem parent of the next problem child. In such situations the child is a very useful 'scapegoat' and blame by parents and society can be transferred to him, causing still further degeneration in the total family environment. In the extreme case the severely impaired child never returns to his parents the independence that 'average' children return when they reach adult status, marry and have their own children. Similarly he cannot offer the practical and emotional support that an adult son or daughter usually offers to older parents. Moreover, the effect is not limited to the family. It spills over into the general social milieu, and studies such as those of Townsend and Jaehnig have shown that the social integration of families with impaired children is poorer than that for parents of normal children. Society rejects not only the handicapped child, but his parents, brothers and sisters as well.

4

The School Years

A child does not suddenly become ready for school on his fifth birthday or achieve pubescence on his eleventh. He mentally and physically grows and develops from infancy to adult life. Certain events, such as puberty, are clearly identified and associated with major physiological or behavioural changes, but we are basically discussing a continuum of development, not a series of discrete events occurring at irregular intervals. Therefore, whilst it would be wrong to imply that the primary school years are a half-way house between infancy and adolescence, these years do represent a period of outgrowth from the pre-school into the adolescent years. The child develops cognitively, emotionally and socially, and the school curriculum needs to be closely geared to this development and to cater to such specific traits as 'the awareness of self' which tends to become apparent in the fifth and sixth year.

Despite the fact that ordinary schools do cater for varying grades of ability and achievement, a number of children require special help over and above that provided for the child who is not handicapped. In January 1976 there were about 177 000 children in England receiving some form of special education, but to set this figure in context it must be remembered that there were over 9·7 million children attending schools of all types. A more detailed breakdown of the nature of this provision is given in Table 7, but this table must not be read as a definite statement of prevalence rates for different disabilities in children. Some disabilities are more likely to require the child to be taught in a special school or class, and there are historical reasons why certain disabilities, such as deafness and blindness, are more likely to result in the child attending a special school. Nevertheless, it is interesting to note that the large bulk (132 000) of children receiving special attention in England are classified as educationally subnormal or physically handicapped. There are local shortages and provision for some disabilities, for example autism, is notoriously low, but over all supply and demand seem to be reasonably in balance, since only 3244 children had been waiting for admission to a special school or class for over a year. We are not suggesting that local or specific shortages should not be rectified, but it would seem that large-scale development of special schools and classes is not required *on the basis of present admission criteria*. Whether or not these criteria are the right ones is more debatable, and an issue that we shall touch upon later in this chapter.

TABLE 7

The number of handicapped children attending or awaiting admission to special schools in England and Wales, January 1976. (Source: Department of Education. 1976. *Statistics of Education.* Vol. I. *Schools.* Table 26. London: HMSO. *Reproduced by permission of the Controller of Her Majesty's Stationery Office*)

	Blind	Partially sighted	Deaf	Partially hearing	Physically handi-capped	Delicate	Mal-adjusted	Educationally sub-normal Medium	Educationally sub-normal Severe	Epileptic	Speech defect	Autistic	Total
Assessment and placement during 1975													
Pupils newly assessed as requiring special educational treatment	120	271	257	515	1 894	1 305	4 310	9 365	2 823	169	294	70	21 393
Pupils newly placed in special schools or boarding homes	124	282	284	544	2 055	1 397	3 911	10 463	3 007	151	278	78	22 574
Handicapped pupils in January 1976													
Attending special schools[1]													
Maintained													
Day pupils	115	1 136	1 574	1 209	9 641	3 273	4 767	54 870	27 981	452	1 094	434	106 546
Boarding pupils	202	418	442	440	1 345	1 629	3 437	6 727	2 685	265	56	91	17 737
Non-maintained													
Day pupils	68	83	255	93	484	4	6	437	10	6	14	25	1 485
Boarding pupils	751	397	1 236	501	1 324	476	1 154	912	145	499	161	32	7 588
Attending designated special classes at maintained primary, middle and secondary schools													
On a full-time basis	—	149	225	2 335	414	167	1 728	12 271	633	91	597	57	18 667
On a part-time basis	—	16	53	914	29	10	149	793	11	4	19	5	2 003
Boarded in homes	1	—	—	1	2	67	478	8	26	1	—	—	584
Attending independent schools under arrangements made by Authorities	15	17	304	98	749	185	4 011	516	616	8	34	216	6 769
Receiving education otherwise than at school[2]	18	16	55	75	1 288	459	2 445	298	1 189	50	54	49	5 996
Awaiting admission to special schools[3]													
Day pupils													
Age 5 and over	5	46	16	56	240	165	356	3 699	416	7	40	8	5 054
Under 5	10	15	23	90	264	18	3	184	760	4	17	4	1 392
Boarding pupils													
Age 5 and over	27	36	34	25	82	234	1 402	635	130	43	43	18	2 709
Under 5	24	20	20	29	25	7	2	15	15	—	13	1	158
All pupils	1 236	2 349	4 237	5 866	15 887	6 694	19 938	81 352	34 617	1 430	2 142	940	176 688
Awaiting admission for more than a year[4]	14	38	26	62	150	116	410	1 945	441	10	21	11	3 244

1 Including attached units and Hospital Special Schools

TABLE 8

Children in the care of local authorities in the year ending 31 March 1976. (Source: Department of Health and Social Security: English statistics, Personal Social Services/Local Authority Statistics. A/F76/12, p. 5; Welsh Office unpublished statistics)

Children in the care of Local Authorities in the year ending 31 March 1976	England Total	Wales Total	England & Wales Total
A) Categories of all children in care: Total	95 786	4 842	100 628
a) Under Section 1 Children Act 1948[1]	6 412	162	6 574
b) Others in care under Section 1 Children Act 1948	40 379	2 065	42 444
c) Under Section 23 of the CYP[2] Act 1969[3]	628	18	646
d) Under an interim order (Sect. 22 CYP Act 1969)	1 163	59	1 222
e) Under a care order	44 254	2 378	46 632
f) Under Section 43(1) of the Matrimonial Causes Act 1973	1 934	133	2 067
g) Under Section 2(1)(e) of the Matrimonial Proceedings (Magistrates' Courts) Act 1960	758	22	780
h) Under Section 7(2) of the Family Law Reform Act 1969	118	—	118
i) Under Section 2(2)(b) of the Guardianship Act 1973	140	5	145
B) Age groups of all children (at 31 March 1976): Total	95 786	4 842	100 628
Under the age of two	3 782	248	4 030
Reached the age of two but not of compulsory school age	7 967	386	8 353
Of compulsory school age	64 887	3 173	68 060
Over compulsory school age	19 150	1 035	20 185

[1] and judged likely to return to their parent or guardian within 6 months of the date of being received into care

[2] CYP: Children and Young Persons Act

[3] or detained in care under Section 29(3) of the 1969 Act

We can also look at the problem of prevalence in another way, and one that perhaps comments on environmental disadvantage, which relates in a more immediate way to social factors rather than to the individual characteristics of the child. Table 8 shows that in England and Wales in 1976, a total of about 101 000 children were in the care of local authorities, and of these about two-thirds were of compulsory school age. The legislation under which children can be taken into care is complex, but it covers two main areas. First, the local authority may, under Section 1 of the Children Act 1948, receive a child into its care where the child has no parents or guardian or has been abandoned, or has parents or a guardian whose circumstances prevent them from taking care of the child. Under Section 2 of that Act the local authority may, by 'resolution', assume the parental rights and duties in relation to a child in their care under Section 1 where the inability or unfitness of the parents or guardian to care for the child themselves satisfies prescribed conditions, which include physical or mental disability or consistent failure without reasonable cause to discharge the obligations of a parent. Second, legal authority to permit courts to commit the child to the care of a local authority is given by a number of Acts, but the children fall into two distinct groups. The first group consists of children for whom the primary focus is on the risk to the child himself; the second group comprises children caught up in matters involving matrimonial dispute and wardship and guardianship which have obvious implications for the care of the child, and, therefore, permit the court to take action to protect him. The primary legal mechanism for dealing with the first type of problem is for the courts to issue a 'care order' under the Children and Young Persons Act (1969), which again vests parental authority in the local authority. This same Act also covers some specific situations which were thought to require special provision. Of particular importance in Table 8, are: (i) Section 22, which allows for interim orders and requires the local authority to return to the court so that the case may be reviewed, and (ii) Sections 23 and 29 which in extreme cases permit the child to be referred to a remand centre or in the absence of such a centre to the remand wing of a prison or to be retained in custody under the care of a local authority. In cases of matrimonial dispute, the appropriate court may place the children of the marriage in the custody of the local authority, thereby removing from the parents the freedom to determine where the child shall live and how he shall spend his time. Finally, although it does not ascribe care to the local authority, it should be mentioned that parents' rights may be removed by the court in adoption proceedings under Section 12 of the Children's Act (1975) when either the parent cannot give agreement to the adoption, or he is unreasonably withholding his agreement, or he is a danger to the child.

Children taken into care do not necessarily require special education; indeed the large majority attend ordinary schools. Nevertheless, they are a group of children as deserving of sympathy as, and often of equal need to those more normally defined as handicapped. Moreover, there is a high association between being taken into care, and being prone to become 'casualties of life' in the adult years. Unsuccessful marriage, involvement with the courts, and low socio-economic status are but three things that are more prevalent for children taken into care, when they become adult. We have included the group in this chapter because their needs are similar in concept if not in detail to those of handicapped children, and the ideas discussed in subsequent paragraphs have relevance for thier care and treatment. Indeed, it is hardly surprising that this is so, since they are the needs of all children, impaired or otherwise, differing only in the detailed modifications of the environment that are necessary if they are to be met.

The learning process

As part of a process of growth and development the child will need during the primary school years to: (i) learn the physical skills necessary for everyday living, (ii) build wholesome attitudes towards himself as a growing organism, (iii) learn to get along with peers, (iv) learn an appropriate sex role, (v) develop fundamental skills in reading, writing and calculating, (vi) develop concepts necessary for everyday living, (vii) develop conscience, morality, and a scale of values, and (viii) develop attitudes towards social groups and institutions (Thorpe & Johnson, 1962). When the child moves into adolescence he enters a transition point at which relationships are restructured:

> adolescents are interesting to know—just because it is a period of transition. A person who is living through any phase of rapid change, in history, in society, in individual development, may thereby be the more interesting, the livelier a person. There is for him the demand, or at least the opportunity, to direct his thoughts both behind and ahead of the present moment; swinging rapidly from one perspective to another, comparing, predicting, regretting and resolving afresh; planning for the future but preserving continuity with the present; making the best of what has been, ensuring the best of what could come (Veness, 1961).

Whether this period of rapid learning takes place at school or elsewhere, informal and formal learning itself functions as a servo-system. The basis of new learning lies in exploratory experiences, but for learning to take place a child must have: (i) adequate previous experience of learning; (ii) exposure to tasks related to fundamental ideas; (iii) an active role for himself; (iv) a context of appropriate concepts; (v) an interesting pattern underlying the surface of every task; (vi) experiences appropriate to his developmental age; and (vii) a sequence of experiences that adds up to something perceived as worthwhile (see Davis, 1967). The breakdown of any parts of the system will impair learning; either it will take place with less than maximum efficiency or it may in extreme cases break down completely. In the rest of this chapter we shall discuss in more detail the ways in which progress may be facilitated and breakdown prevented, but since we are adopting a psycho-social perspective we shall have little to say about the school curriculum itself. We shall concentrate on those general problems that are predeterminants of whether or not a good curriculum will permit a child to learn.

Environmental mastery

Schools are agents in the socialization of the child, and particularly so in the case of the handicapped child. The very young child has little control over his environment and, therefore, little concept of self. He does not know where he ends and where the world begins, and only through physical contact is he able to identify with objects outside of himself. At a later stage the child develops greater control over the environment and functions more autonomously, but to do so he must first achieve mastery of the environment which requires that from a young age he should receive an appropriate programme of social education and training. For most of us this programme is coincidental with other activities, and there has been little analytical thought given to how it is that normal children grow up into relatively normal adults.

We know the school and family are important, we know something about how they influence development, and we are learning to improve the techniques that we use in child-rearing and in education. Nevertheless, one of our problems in working with handicapped and disabled children and adults is that we do not really know how the environment operates on the individual. We see the environmental effects negatively, as in a greater incidence of delinquency in socially deprived areas, a greater incidence of malnutrition in less developed countries, and in the adopting of socially unacceptable forms of behaviour by large groups of individuals in times of social upheaval and stress such as war. The negatives are clear but the positives are not; we do not know why some children in the same environment do not become delinquent, why some children recover from malnutrition, and why some people do not engage in socially unacceptable forms of behaviour even though they are apparently subject to the same stressful environment.

Despite our limited knowledge about how to achieve mastery of the environment, we can illustrate in Figure 10 the desirable characteristics of a programme leading to optimum development of handicapped and disabled children. The same programme will be equally applicable for those who become handicapped or disabled later in life, but the point at which they start in the programme may be different, as indeed it will be different for each individual child. Stimulation by language and other means in the early years of life is the starting-point for the development of dependency or independency and it begins with the family. We are not arguing that at whatever cost the child should remain with his natural family. Indeed, there are situations where for his own protection he-will need to be removed from an inadequate psychological home environment, although it is important to remember that the physical effects of the environment are more important by their influence on the parents' mental health than on their direct effect on the psychological state of the child.

The depression of poverty affects some but not all parents to such a degree that the family is unable to adopt good child-rearing techniques and it may even place the child in physical danger. When this occurs society must consider the child's need for protection and consider whether or not he should be taken into care. However, taking a child into care because of poor housing conditions alone, and certainly taking him into care because we are unable or unwilling to provide the family with a decent home, is dangerously short-sighted. The eventual costs to the health, education and social services will far exceed the cost of providing a home without including the hidden costs of the loss of productive potential when the child becomes an adult. Moreover, the only form of care which, at the moment, seems to be reasonably successful includes the provision of good surrogate parents, be they kindly relatives, hard-working house parents in family-based small group homes, or formal or informal adoptive parents. Other techniques, such as placing children in short-term foster care, do not seem able to replace the natural or adoptive family of the child and they do little to prevent social or emotional maladjustment. Whatever we do in later years, the child's first environment is crucial, and if we fail him then his development will be less effective. It will be extremely hard to overcome the effects of such early deprivation, although the effects are not as static or as irreversible as is sometimes thought to be the case (see Rutter & Madge, 1976, for a review of this whole field). Some children who have been deprived in the pre-school and the school years go on to be successful, but a large majority do not, and the question always remains as to whether those who have been 'successful' would have been more successful if their earlier experiences had been more favourable.

The Gunzburgs' model

At the other end of the continuum of development we have the aim of enabling the disabled or handicapped person to live in the open community. Success in achieving this goal will depend crucially on the degree to which we have provided appropriate education and training,

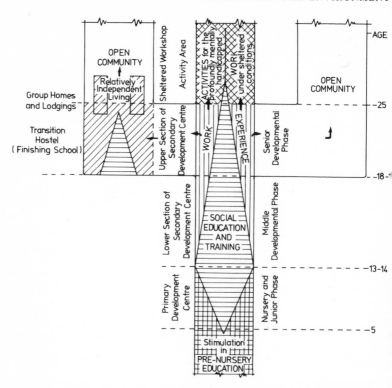

FIGURE 10   A social education and training programme for handicapped children and adults, and its physical environment. (Source: Gunzburg, H. C. & Gunzburg, Anna L. 1973. *Mental Handicap and Physical Environment*. London: Baillière Tindall)

and the Gunzburgs have placed considerable emphasis on this aspect of the problem. Herbert Charles Gunzburg is Director of Psychological Services in the Mental Subnormality Division of a large hospital in the Midlands of Britain. He and his wife, Anna, have worked extensively on the problems of the remedial teaching of mentally handicapped patients. They brought their experience to bear on these problems in a recent book *Mental Handicap and Physical Environment*, which emphasized the better operational planning of environments for the mentally handicapped. The book starts with a theme taken from President J. F. Kennedy's 'National Plan to Combat Mental Retardation', viz. that specific preventive measures 'would eliminate perhaps half or more of all the new cases of mental retardation'. A similar theme is taken in the Department of Health and Social Security's consultative document published in 1976, *Prevention and Health: Everybody's Business*, although in this case the emphasis is on health in general and not specific problems of disability or of the mentally handicapped. Instead of describing schools, training centres or similar institutions, the Gunzburgs describe what they refer to as 'development centres' (Figure 10). In such a structure, development flows naturally through various stages into work experience, a vital emphasis because in our society it is often forgotten that the unemployed or the unemployable suffer from severe social stigma and stand little hope of achieving environmental mastery even at a physical, let alone a social or a psychological, level. Productive employment does not guarantee that we can buy an adequate physical environment, but without it or without income from some other source there is little doubt that we shall spend most of our lives in physically inadequate conditions.

To prevent deterioration or a failure to develop, education and training needs to concentrate on four major areas: (i) self-help; (ii) education; (iii) communication, and (iv) socialization. Self-help involves developing skills of physical self-sufficiency, skills of self-control and skills of self-care. Education is not to be confused with work although oftentimes for adolescents work-related activities are useful ways of developing occupational skills. Skills in this area relate to the ability to function as a mental, psychological or social stimulus to oneself and to others. Communication skills are those skills that enable us to relate to the world that surrounds us. Socialization is the process whereby skills are developed that enable us to function as social animals living in a group setting. It includes the acquisition of abstract concepts of ethics and morality as well as relatively simpler concepts such as the appropriate behaviour when lining up for and catching a bus. It is tempting, but it would be wrong to equate mastery of the environment with socialization. Self-help is concerned with a physically more limited environment, but it still demands the ability to manipulate and control. Any individual cannot be adequately socialized unless he is able to control himself autonomously and at the same time influence those who surround and interact with him in his wider environment.

The model developed by the Gunzburgs (1973) from their work with mentally handicapped children and adults can be profitably used with all types of handicap and even with so-called normal individuals. There are specific effects associated with specific disabilities, such as the walk of the spastic. Such effects are still best remediated by looking in the first instance at the development of the impaired skill in those who are unimpaired. For certain disabled or handicapped people we may have to put considerable emphasis on a remedial programme designed to help them overcome the specific aspects of their disability, and the techniques and skills developed may differ from those used by non-impaired children. A good example is the person who becomes hearing-impaired in later life. Until he is impaired to a degree where hearing no longer functions adequately he will have the same kind of developmental experience and develop in the same way as an unimpaired person. When the loss of hearing becomes significant, intensive and specific teaching will be needed to develop lip-reading skills and to retain speech that is reasonably normally articulated. These very specific problems do not invalidate the Gunzburgs' analysis. The ability to perform in a psycho-social environment will be affected by the hearing impairment, often seriously so, and without help autonomous control through mastery of the environment will be more limited than it has been in the past. Training in lip-reading and speech will not overcome, it will only reduce, these effects. The same problem arises even more with disabled people or children whose handicap developed at birth or early in life, but in this case it is less easy to differentiate the specific and developmental causes. The retarded child should be regarded as a child who has developed mentally but who has not progressed at the same rate as a 'normal' child. He is sometimes regarded as a child subject to a known or unknown medical condition which results in special difficulties in performing intellectual tasks and coping socially. The difference may not seem very important, but it has had significant effects on our perception of handicapped people and explains why it was not until 1969 that Junior Training Centres for severely subnormal adolescents in Britain were seen as an educational rather than a health service.

A specific example

We can illustrate the principles underlying the previous discussion by a specific example—mobility training in blind children and adults. The different phases in the achievement of optimum mobility have been described by Cratty and Sams (1968) and are illustrated in Figure 11. A failure to provide an earlier skill prevents the development of a later one, and at whatever the age the child or adult starts training he will have to progress systematically through each stage. Body image will be achieved by activities such as rolling on mats, feeling and manipulating his own body, feeling and manipulating other people's bodies, maze learning, rhythmic games and similar activities. Once the child has a clear mental image of his own body he can progress to organizing perceptually his spatial environment, through tasks such as object matching, sorting by shape and texture, and relating together objects with complementary functions. The next stage of development is to an abstract cognitive representation of an unseen world, most clearly exemplified in the ability to organize and interpret symbolic cues on a tactile map. Finally, if all the earlier skills exist the child or adult can

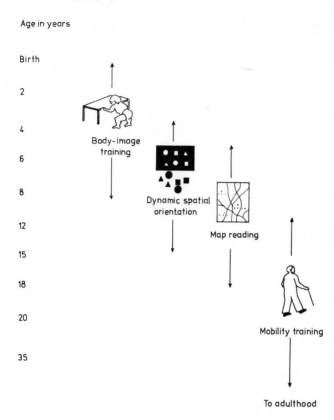

Age in years

Birth

2

4

6

8

12

15

18

20

35

Body-image training

Dynamic spatial orientation

Map reading

Mobility training

To adulthood

FIGURE 11   The steps required to achieve optimum mobility for a congenitally blind child. Knowledge of orientation in space and ability to represent such orientation mentally are necessary prerequisites to mobility. (Based on Cratty, B. J. & Sams, T. A. 1968. *The Body-Image of Blind Children*. New York: American Foundation for the Blind)

make the translation to a real world in which tactile, kinesthetic and auditory cues replace visual ones, and by so doing will achieve reasonable freedom of movement in the home, the school and the community at large.

Institutions

The oldest special schools are schools for blind children, and the history of the institutionalization of children and adults is well documented. The effects of many such institutions on the development of their inmates are vividly portrayed in a poem by George Crabbe quoted in Norman Longmate's fascinating and detailed documentary on *The Workhouse*:

> Your plan I love not. With a number you
> Have placed your poor, your pitiable few;
> There, in one house, throughout their lives to be,
> The pauper-palace which they hate to see:
> That giant-building, that high-bounding wall,
> Those bare-worn walks, that lofty thundering hall!
> That large loud clock, which tolls each dreaded hour,
> Those gates and locks and all those signs of power:
> It is a prison, with a milder name,
> Which few inhabit without dread or shame.

The medical model of the times had much influence on workhouse practices because, analogously to a disease, the inmates were thought to be constitutionally endowed with some defective capacity which prevented their leading an industrious life. It provided the theoretical justification for much damaging practice because it aimed to provide treatment for the untreatable. It saw handicap as a specific disability and in consequence any progress that resulted in less than 'perfection' was regarded as a failure. In contrast, a recent major study by Miller and Gwynne (1973), called *A Life Apart*, differentiates between what the authors call the warehousing and the horticultural techniques. The original perspective of the workhouse no longer exists but Miller and Gwynne vividly contrast these two types of care. The 'horticultural' approach involves working with the residents of an institution to enable them to develop themselves to their full capacity. In a 'warehouse' the emphasis is on placing the resident into his proper 'slot'—a slot that is geared more to the needs of the institution than to those of the resident. Like the workhouse it is a situation that of necessity creates a feeling of futility and failure. None of us works well in situations of failure, and the environment of an institution which sees handicap primarily as a specific disability becomes unstimulating for both residents and staff. It creates low expectations of the possible potential achievements of disabled and handicapped children and adults, and the failure to appreciate the difference between knowing the specific causes of a disability and knowing what are the environmental consequences of that disability has led to some highly dangerous assumptions.

For example, much fruitless discussion about the relative importance of heredity and environment in determining an individual's level of intelligence has been conducted in a situation of social inequalities which precluded any serious experimental manipulation of the second main variable. The question certainly cannot be resolved in this context by reference to patchy and incomplete attempts at environmental engineering which rely on extra teaching for a few hours a week or a few weeks in the year, such as are undertaken under the 'Headstart' programme in the USA and Educational Priority Areas in Great Britain. Such programmes mostly fail because limited exposure to environmental advantage is insufficient to undo the severe damage caused by the previous and usually continuing environmental disadvantage. Their failure does not call into question the wisdom of providing positive discrimination or indeed the nature of the positive discrimination provided. It does call into question social policies which assume that it is possible to overcome the multiple effects of economic, social, familial and environmental deprivation by relatively tiny doses of *preventive* treatment *after* the main damage has been done. To provide educational priority programmes without at the same time providing social, cultural and physical priority programmes is to so handicap the programmes that they are doomed to failure.

It was concern with the disabling social, psychological and educational effects of a poor environment that led to the establishment of Office of Economic Opportunity and 'Headstart' programmes in the United States and to the Urban Aid Programmes and the Educational Priority Areas in Britain. The educational provision concentrated relatively large sums of public money on providing innovative and experimental programmes for deprived children, including a small number who were handicapped. The other types of programme were more broadly based but had essentially the same concept. Special public funds were earmarked to be made available to provide innovative social programmes in areas thought to be of high need.

Individual projects within both the British and the American programmes have been successful in producing change either in the children involved or in general social awareness and organization. However, the consensus of opinion is that both programmes have mainly failed in their original concept, namely that intensive aid would result in major and long-lasting change. Holman (1973, our italics) has suggested some basic questions the answers to which may indicate why, as he says of the British programme:

> Neither [*political party*] concedes or even discusses the point
> that to concentrate services on changing the deprived will be
> of limited value if the causes of deprivation rest mainly in the
> social structures of society, rather than in the personalities of
> the poor, or in their *immediate* environment. The emphasis
> on better socialising experiences for children will avail little if

schools are required to maintain present hierarchies *by ensuring that some children fail*. The counselling or training of parents into different forms of behaviour will have little outcome if the public and private housing market is such that some people must be '*selected' for*, or 'rationed' into private slums or local authority sub-standard property. Increased job training will mean little in the situation where institutionalised occupational prejudice operates against the handicapped.

In other words, why change people if the opportunities for them to change their role are unchanged? Indeed, if poverty results from factors outside the control of the poor, a reaction of despising school, lacking motivation to work, and refusing to conform to more conventional standards of behaviour may be regarded as a rational adaptation to intolerable circumstances rather than the direct result of inadequate childhood socialization experiences.

Integration

A basically three-tier system operates in the education of handicapped children. At one extreme we have independent, autonomous special schools where the child is educated with children having a similar type of handicap. At the other extreme we have children who receive their education in ordinary schools with 'normal' children, sometimes with but often without special individual help. In between the two we have established within ordinary schools special classes or units in which the handicapped child spends all or part of his school day. Teachers and other professional groups disagree among themselves as to which of these systems is 'best', possibly because the amount of objective evidence available to answer the question is limited.

It is claimed that the advantage of special schools is that they provide empathy between the environment and the needs of the handicapped child; they provide a concentration of expertise; they permit in residential schools twenty-four hours a day remedial treatment; and that by grouping children into larger units they enable them to be divided more equitably into equal ability and equal need groups; that they permit children to partake in activities which provide the emotional and social support that comes from a clear sub-cultural identity; that they provide concentrated training in specific skills related to the handicapped; and that a sense of belonging provides the best basis for the child to enter the complex world of adult life. In contrast proponents of integrating handicapped children into ordinary classes argue that the ordinary school provides real experiences for the child, and that such experience will better prepare the child for life outside the school; that more specialist educational resources are available to the child because ordinary schools must and can provide greater academic and vocational choices; that by separating the child you emphasize his or her differences whereas integration into a regular class minimizes these differences; that teachers used to working with 'normal' children are better able to evaluate the child's progress and development; and that the standards of teachers working in regular schools will not become depressed by working continuously with a disadvantaged group. The protagonists of special classes in regular schools combine the arguments of both camps and claim that it is possible to have the best of both worlds.

It is unfortunate that energy is wasted on the often heated arguments about which kind of school is best. We need facilities that are complementary rather than competitive. Anderson (1973), whose study of physically handicapped children receiving education in ordinary primary schools in England was exceptionally searching, concludes that 'given special provisions . . . it is possible to offer even severely handicapped children a satisfactory education in an ordinary school'. She considers, however, that 'for certain children special schools may always be needed, but as the provision of special educational treatment within ordinary schools increases, this need is likely to be smaller than at present'. She suggests three main functions for the special schools:

> The first is that they should be used increasingly as observation and assessment centres. Secondly they should provide children (from as early an age as possible) with an initial period of skilled and intensive training by teachers and therapists working together. . . . After this period, which might for some children last from one to four years, many children would be ready for transfer to a special or ordinary class. Ideally the special school would be sited close to an ordinary school so that for at least part of the time handicapped and non-handicapped children could be taught in mixed groups. Thirdly, special schools could act as advisory centres from which . . . experienced teachers and therapists could travel as consultants to teachers in special and ordinary classes who need help.

There are also practical reasons for retaining more than one type of special facility. Unlike the present situation when the large majority of children 'track' for the whole of their school careers in one type of facility, movement between different types of facility needs to be simplified so that as their needs change children can be transferred between differing facilities offering differing types of environment. There is no need for a well-adjusted blind or deaf child who is living in a large urban area with an intact family to attend a residential school. There is a need in such areas for special facilities of a residential type to meet the needs of small groups such as deaf/blind children, behaviourally disturbed retarded children, or other multiply handicapped and very severely subnormal children. Whatever type of facility we are talking about, more thought and planning has to be given to what some might regard as the non-educational aspects of the programme, but which are really the basis of all education. Schools of all types frequently negate their educational aims by failing to attend to the psychological principles of good child-rearing, social development and the processes of group interaction. Ten-bed dormitories and untrained house parents have no place in modern educational institutions, but both still exist. Failure to provide good programmes of social development, including sex and drug education, is even more regrettable. Integration will not occur simply because of proximity, and to ignore the problems of the handicapped child in coping with his or her handicap is to ignore all that we have learned about attitudes and the need to 'educate' communities if 'good' attitudes are to be developed—that is, the environmental effects of disability.

5

The Middle Years

It is right that we as a society should give very serious attention to the education and preparation for life of disabled children. It is wrong that we should and do show relatively less concern for the needs of those children when they grow up and for the very much larger group of people who become disabled in adult life. For each physically impaired child receiving or awaiting admission to special educational treatment in Britain today, there are at least 50 people over the age of 16, living in their own homes, who fall into Amelia Harris's categories of 'very severely' or 'severely' handicapped. In addition, Harris's estimates suggest that for every disabled child another 60 adults are suffering from 'appreciable' handicap while nearly 200 more have minor impairments resulting in little or no immediate handicap.*

Amelia Harris's estimates of the total number of physically impaired adults living at home in Great Britain is a little over 3 million, which includes in the very severely, severely and appreciably handicapped categories nearly 400 000 people of working age (16–64) and upwards of 730 000 people aged 65 and over. As handicapped school-leavers grow older they become lost in the statistics of disability, among those who have acquired disability through accidents or illnesses in the middle years of life. As late middle and old age approach increasing numbers of newly disabled people owe their handicaps to such chronic afflictions as arthritis and rheumatism, diseases of the respiratory system (including

---

* While the statistics available for child and adult handicap are for several reasons not strictly comparable, this rough comparison has been arrived at as follows: Harris's (1971, p. 18) study of the degree of handicap of impaired people in different age groups and estimated numbers in Great Britain living at home has been used for adults. This very detailed survey was concerned primarily with motor disorders that make it difficult or impossible for people to look after themselves without help (getting dressed, washing, eating and drinking, etc.). Sensory impairment (with the exception of blindness), communication difficulties, and mental illness or handicap therefore tended to fall outside the scope of the study. In comparing Harris's figures with the DES (1973) *Statistics of Education*, vol. 1, *Schools* (p. 60) which is concerned with the school population in January 1972, children receiving or awaiting admission to special educational treatment for hearing impairments, speech defects, educational subnormality maladjustment and those in hospital schools were excluded, but an adjustment was made to include children below school age. While it is known that many handicapped children attend ordinary schools, it is unlikely that any but a very small minority of children with handicaps comparable to Harris's 'severe' and 'very severe' categories were at ordinary schools at the time covered by the statistics.

chronic bronchitis) and of the heart and circulatory system, and to cerebral haemorrhages and strokes.

The comparison between the numbers of handicapped children and adults in the community offers only a rough guide to the comparative size of the problems. Also, it does not warn us of differences in the pattern of handicap in the two populations. It made sense, for instance, for Harris to exclude the figures for so-called 'mental subnormality' from the comparison, although by far the largest group of children referred for special education (nearly 70 per cent) are classified as Educationally Subnormal (ESN). Of these, probably only a minority are being educated as ESN (severe), the majority being in schools or units for the ESN (mild). Indeed many, although by no means all, young people labelled ESN (M) in their school years later settle comfortably into the adult community, holding down jobs in open employment, marrying and bringing up families as successfully as anyone else. Heavier demands are made upon intellectual ability in school than most people ever experience in adult life and the children classified as ESN (M) constitute strong support for the hypothesis that much of the behaviour we label 'abnormal' is a function of the environment rather than of the individual (see also Dexter, 1958).

Psychology of the social environment

A useful approach to understanding the nature of the relationship between a person who has been categorized 'disabled' and his social environment is found in the psychological concept of 'life-space' as developed by Lewin (1951). This concept is illustrated graphically in Figure 12. Each individual is shown as having a private life-space which he inhabits alone and a public life-space which he shares with others. His private life-space is not a geographical area in the real world, but it is the individual's private conception of the universe of space and time in which he can or might move about either physically or in imagination, thought, or memory. It includes his own perceptions of his immediate experiences and his knowledge (true and false) and values and expectations and ideas of the past and the future, and of himself in relation to all these and to other people. It is entirely his own and is quite different from the private life-space of anyone else. In his public life-space, however, he has come to terms with others, to share ideas and values, as in a formal meeting where all accept assigned roles and behave very differently from when they are at home. There is of course no real boundary between private and public life-space: our private beliefs do influence our public role-playing and vice versa. Hence the frontier may be for the individual dangerous ground where internal

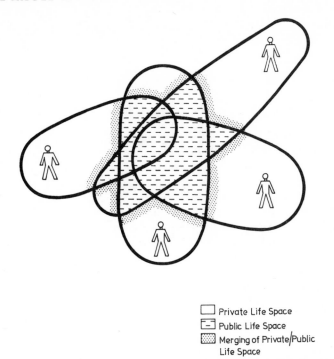

☐ Private Life Space
⊟ Public Life Space
▦ Merging of Private/Public
   Life Space

FIGURE 12   Diagram illustrating Lewin's concept of life-space, the boundaries of
which are our physical environment. (Based on Lewin, K. 1951. *Field Theory in Social
Science*. New York: Harper & Row)

conflicts may arise between the free attitudes and emotions of his
private life-space and the constraints of his public one. The situation is
further complicated when we consider that all individuals are members
of several different groups (for example at home, at work, at leisure),
each demanding different patterns of identification. In a well-known
passage Lewin ascribed the 'difficulties of adolescence' to the young
person's inability to make a smooth and easy transference from
membership of the childhood group, which he has outgrown, to the
adult group, still unwilling to accept him fully. He is in a position similar
to that occupied by what sociologists term the 'marginal man'. The
marginal man stands on a boundary between two groups, belonging to
neither, or at least uncertain about his belongingness. Lewin himself
extends this comparison from adolescents to minority groups in
general, and mentions specifically such people as the hard of hearing,
whom he describes as a marginal group between the deaf and the
normally hearing. The concept has wider relevance in a democratic
culture that stresses 'ordinariness' as a positive quality. It is very

difficult to accept the classification 'disabled' and conceptualize oneself consistently as a member of an 'abnormal' group.

The predicament of the newly disabled

The concept of 'life-space' may also help us to understand an important distinction between the handicapping effects of a congenital impairment and one that is acquired in adult life. The distinction may be illustrated in this way: one of the writers has two friends, both without sight, and from time to time may give either of them a lift by car. Neither is an easy passenger. One is keenly interested in what is going on outside the car and asks questions continuously—'Which way are we going? Where are we now? Is there a lot of traffic about?' The other, who lost his sight in infancy, continues to pursue with scarcely enough break to settle himself in his seat, an animated discussion of whatever ideas were occupying his mind before the journey began. On one occasion when giving a lift to the second, the driver, having twice got into the wrong lane of traffic through trying to respond at the right level and simultaneously navigate the car through London, remarked on this difference between the two. 'Oh,' said the friend, 'but that's easy to explain. Tom is really a sighted man.' Tom's private life-space, he implied, is still in many ways the same as it was before he lost his sight as a very young man. He represents the world to himself visually. He orients his activities within a visual world that he can no longer see but seeks continuously to reconstruct in his 'mind's eye'. To John who cannot remember sight, the world of ideas and human relationships is sufficient. What goes on outside a car is usually just a bore.

The environmental problem that confronts the newly disabled adult is then in some respects the reverse of the impaired child's. For the child, and for his friends and teachers, there is continuous, conscious effort to extend the boundaries of his life-space to bring him nearer to the world of his unimpaired contemporaries. One effect of this may be to emphasize his marginality as he approaches adolescence. Indeed, he is doubly marginal: a child unassimilated to the adult world, but also increasingly aware of his difference from its average members. The newly disabled adult, however, expends much effort in a struggle to hold back the boundaries of his life-space, both private and public, which seem to be perpetually shrinking. For many the introduction to disability is a slow but not a gradual process. Following the realization that health, sight or hearing are 'not what they were' there may be a long period of mounting anxiety punctuated by several postponed decisions to seek professional advice. Too often there may be further delays before a diagnosis is made and treatment prescribed. There may follow a measure of remission and adjustment to use of aids, but this can be the prelude to a long night of fear until the anticipated moment is reached when independent functioning breaks down and with it the old way of life. For others, the victims of injuries or sudden acute disabling illnesses, disability occurs without warning. In either case, with the onset of disability the old familiar life-space in which the now-disabled person could once move easily and confidently slips away from him. All his strategies for living, his perceptions and ways of thinking, as well as his behaviour in the physical and social environment, were valid only in the context of the old world. They cannot stand alone. They were in fact relationships with known points in that world. It is not simply that his processes and actions are restricted in its absence. Without it he may for a time be unable to act at all.

This experience has been vividly described by Linduska (1947):

> But suddenly I woke up one morning, and found that I could not stand. I had had polio, and polio was as simple as that. I was like a very young child who had been dropped into a big, black hole, and the only thing I was certain of was that I could not get out unless someone helped me. The education, the lectures, the parental training which I had received for twenty-four years didn't seem to make me the person who could do anything for me now. I was like everyone else—normal, quarrelsome, gay, full of plans, and all of a sudden something happened! Something happened and I became a stranger. I was a greater stranger to myself than to anyone. Even my dreams did not know me. They did not know what they ought to let me do—and when I went to dances or to parties in them, there was always an odd provision or limitation—not spoken of or mentioned, but there just the same. I suddenly had the very confusing mental and emotional conflict of a lady leading a double life. . . .

Festinger's (1957) theory of cognitive dissonance provides a useful framework for looking at the consequences of this kind of conflict. It can also help us to understand why the man in the street or the wife, husband, son or daughter in the handicapped person's home may frequently adopt inappropriate and often derogatory attitudes towards the disabled. The theory maintains that if a person knows various things that are not psychologically consistent with one another he will be strongly motivated to make them more consistent. To attempt to organize one's actions in the light of two sets of apparent facts ('dissonant items of information') is in itself an uncomfortable and potentially disabling condition. The items of information may be about the environment, or about one's own notions of how one should act, or about one's expectations, opinions, and feelings. Linduska 'knew' that she was the kind of person who dances at parties. The information came from the strongest possible source: her lifelong experience of herself. However, when she tried to stand, rival information from her own body told her that even this was impossible, her only recourse being to fall back into the 'big black hole' of total dependence. But the old objective environment persisted, continuously informing her that doors are there to be opened, floors to be danced upon. So she was compelled to swing between dissonant poles until an input of new information enabled her, slowly, to build a new unitary self-image based upon the sort of life-space she would be able to inhabit in the future.

A crisis of dissonance is likely also to affect the families, friends and casual acquaintances of the newly disabled. The wife of a man recently paralysed by a stroke who knows that her husband is 'really' an active and vigorous man may harbour unreasonable expectations about his recovery rate and treat him virtually as a malingerer. Alternatively she may accept the seeming evidence of her senses and reclassify him as a helpless burden. Clearly, both husband and wife need a rapid input of detailed and realistic information about his recovery prospects, about what they can do to expedite his rehabilitation, about appliances and aids that may help him to compensate for any permanent impairment, and about short- and long-term goals to replace such parts of his old way of life as may no longer be open to him. A delayed start to the rehabilitation programme may have permanent physical, psychological and social effects. As Mattingly (1974) points out, 'if a paralysed arm of the hemiplegic patient is not put passively through a full range of movements each day during the first few weeks after a stroke he will develop a frozen shoulder which may persist for months or even years'. Similarly if he and his wife resolve their problem by accepting his helplessness, changed attitudes to each other may become psychologically 'frozen' in a way damaging not only to his prospects of rehabilitation but also to their future relationship with each other. The first step towards rehabilitation has been taken when the impaired person himself initiates an action resulting in a satisfying change in his environment.

The achievement of environmental mastery by an impaired adult

Environmental mastery implies an environment capable of being changed by its would-be master. To exercise a choice implies an environment that can be altered in more ways than one. Personal autonomy implies the possibility of planning sequences of change in the confidence that desired goals can be achieved. All children soon learn, of course, that total mastery of the environment is an impossible dream: even Canute could not command the sea. Nevertheless, the mature adults in our culture confidently assert the right to make choices in the pursuit of personal goals. We call this 'the right to freedom' and it is one of our most treasured values.

Some of the choices open to the unimpaired are inevitably closed to the severely impaired. A man paralysed by a stroke cannot play tennis, at least while he remains paralysed. It should be remembered, however, that playing tennis is an option cheerfully rejected in favour of others by a great many people who are physically capable of playing, including some who might like to play but lack necessary experience or skill. It is in exercising choice, in arranging priorities by reference to his own needs, the needs of others and the constraints of the situation, that a person demonstrates his maturity. Integration does not imply that every conceivable option open to all unimpaired people can be made equally available to every impaired person. It does demand, however, that there should be a sufficient range of options open to any impaired individual to enable him to function as a mature person and pursue a personal life-style as satisfying in its own way as his neighbour's.

The first aim of any rehabilitation programme must be to ensure that every possible step, surgical, medical and therapeutic, is taken to restore as much natural function as possible; the second aim must be to provide the best available prosthetics, appliances and personal aids to maximize residual functioning. These are jobs for professionals working directly with and for the client. In most advanced countries the rehabilitation services go further than this and attempt with varying degrees of success also to slot the individual back into society with either a 'suitable' job in open employment or, if he is considered 'unsuitable' for any of the jobs on offer, with some occupation in a sheltered, separate environment. However, as we have already seen (page 11) the professional services are by their nature incapable of initiating environmental changes of the kind or on the scale necessary for achieving the aim of true integration into the community for large numbers of disabled people. This must be the responsibility of the wider community itself.

Integration and income

The aim of rehabilitation is often said to be resettlement. It is an aim that requires close examination. At its best it implies what we have called full integration; at its worst it may mean no more than getting a problem off the professional's hands and into somebody else's. This latter is the safest recipe for creating a hostile environment. Integration requires the active involvement of the community at all levels. It means a recognition by the public at large of its responsibility towards its handicapped adult members and a clear understanding of their needs and how they can be met. All human societies unquestioningly accept responsibility for certain categories of people who can contribute little or nothing to the economic life of the community. These generally include the very young and the very old. In advanced societies, the tendency has been to extend the period of permitted dependency or semi-dependency at both ends of life. In our culture there is no shame attached to being a school-child or a pensioner.

The cornerstone of adult independence is an adequate personal income. As we have seen in Chapter 2, there is no legislation in Britain concerned specifically with pension rights for all disabled people. The present pattern of provision has developed historically in a variety of ways. Incomes are derived from a number of different sources and include:

1. Sickness, industrial injury and disablement benefits paid to workers who have contributed to the National Insurance Scheme.
2. Statutory 'war pensions and allowances' paid to people whose disability was acquired while serving in HM Forces.
3. Means-tested supplementary benefits and allowances paid to any person disabled or otherwise whose income from other sources falls below a specified minimum.
4. Special allowances and grants, such as the mobility allowance designed to increase the mobility of disabled people, and the attendance allowance designed to facilitate the care of children who require constant attention from their parents as a result of their disability.
5. Payments from private insurance schemes (as in the case of the victims of road accidents).
6. A variety of special or discretionary grants from public or charitable sources, to meet particular needs, perhaps the best known of which is the 'Family Fund', a state-provided source of support for meeting the additional costs of disability which is administered by a voluntary agency, the Joseph Rowntree Memorial Trust.

As a result of this diversity organizations of disabled people such as Disability Alliance now argue for civil pensions related to the degree of disability or loss of earning capacity to replace the complex network of statutory and private benefits, which it is claimed are in many cases insufficient to ward off poverty and rarely compensate adequately for loss or reduction of earning power which follows the onset of disability in adult life. This is not the place to argue in detail the merits or demerits of particular schemes. The point we are making is simply that it is a *community* responsibility to remove the stigma that is often attached to the acceptance of public funds by asserting the *right* of disabled people to adequate support, whether or not they are able to do a full day's work in open employment and irrespective of whether this support is provided through statutory or voluntary means. The realization of this right is a matter for the community, and cannot be shelved by simply asking for government action, although such action can and does help.

Work and disability

Most disabled adults subscribe to the common conviction identified by Warren and discussed in Chapter 1 that '. . . earnings or housework (are) the only socially acceptable roles for people between leaving school and retirement age'. More than economics is involved in the right to work: status, occupation, companionship and a sense of belonging, the opportunity to exercise skills and to hope for advancement are all associated with following one's trade or profession. In Britain as long ago as 1943, the Tomlinson Committee recommended that the only really satisfactory form of resettlement for a disabled person was employment that he could take or keep on his merits as a worker 'in normal competition with his fellows', and this philosophy still guides the employment resettlement services in this and most advanced countries today. We could not quarrel with this as an objective if we could be satisfied that the rules of the competition were fair for all competitors.

Table 9 makes it clear that this solution is not in fact open to a large proportion of disabled people. Of those disabled people classified in the table as 'employable', less than half of the under-fifties were 'working', and only 31 per cent of those aged fifty or over.

The Department of Employment, basing its estimates upon its own records which include a wider range of disabilities than those used in the Social Survey reported in Table 9, considers that there are probably as many as 1·2 million disabled people capable of employment and willing to work, of whom about one million are working. Many of those not working are among those classified in the Social Survey as 'at home' (i.e. not in the employment field). About 13 500 of the employed are in subsidized sheltered employment where wage rates are lower than the trade union rates for workers in comparable trades.

In spite of the discrepancy between the two sets of estimates it is clear that the aim of resettlement in open employment is not being achieved for very large numbers of disabled people; and where it is achieved it

TABLE 9

The working status estimated to nearest 1000 of disabled men and
women aged 16–64 years in Great Britain. (Source: Buckle, T. R.
1971. *Work and Housing of Impaired Persons in Great Britain*
[*Handicapped and Impaired in Great Britain*, Part 2]. Table 7.
London: HMSO. *Reproduced by permission of the Controller of
Her Majesty's Stationery Office*)

		Total	% of total
Working	(635 000	493 000	38
Unemployed	employment	49 000	4
Temporarily	field)		
sick		93 000	7
Occupation centre		11 000	1
Housewife		271 000	21
Retired	(637 000	78 000	6
Permanently	at home)		
disabled unable		291 000	23
to work again			
Total		1 286 000	100

Estimates are to the nearest 1000

may be at a high cost to the individual and the conditions may fall far
short of fair and equal terms.

It is because of these problems that in Britain a special service for
disabled people seeking employment is administered nationally by the
Employment Service Agency, through its nationwide network of Job
Centres. At each such centre a trained Disablement Resettlement
Officer (DRO) is assigned the task of advising disabled applicants and
assisting them to find suitable work. Such applicants need not be
'registered' but the DRO is required, under the terms of the Disabled
Persons (Employment) Act, 1944, to maintain a voluntary register of
people with disabilities expected to last at least twelve months and
sufficient to handicap them substantially in obtaining work. According
to Department of Employment estimates, based upon recent medical
surveys, the number of employed non-registered but eligible disabled
people who have preferred to waive the advantages of registration
rather than incur its perceived stigma probably exceeds the number of
'registered' employees. However, registration does carry three
advantages:

1. *First choice of employment in certain 'designated' types of work.*
   At present these are limited to two: car park attendant and
   passenger lift operator.

2. *Sheltered employment for people capable of work but incapable of maintaining productivity at the level required in open employment.* Most 'sheltered' workers are employed in small workshops set up and subsidized by the government, a local authority and/or a charitable organization. A few belong to group schemes for home-based workers (mainly blind) or are grouped in 'enclaves' under their own special supervisor in an ordinary factory or other open employment situation. Only in the case of enclave workers (whose salaries are subsidized to satisfy trade union agreements) do the incomes of sheltered workers correspond to union levels.

3. *Participation in the Quota Scheme.* This scheme affects the largest number of registered workers. The Act requires that any employer with a workforce of twenty or more workers must, if the proportion of registered disabled people on his staff falls below 3 per cent, accept registered disabled people for all vacancies until his quota is reached again—provided that suitable applicants can be found. The system can be abused. In the final analysis the judge of 'suitability' is always the employer himself and the DRO must provide a permit to employ an able-bodied worker if no suitable disabled candidate is forthcoming. Most DROs prefer persuasion to threats of prosecution and try to build up good relationships with sympathetic employers, arguing, probably correctly, that compulsion is not a good basis for a happy and lasting work relationship. Many large firms are chronically 'below quota' but prosecutions are rare. Nevertheless, the shadow the law casts over the situation almost certainly facilitates the DRO's task.

DROs, however, have other resources to draw upon. In the case of newly disabled people it is important that a DRO should participate as early as possible in planning the rehabilitation programme and it is increasingly becoming the practice for medical consultants to invite a DRO to meet the patient while he is still in hospital. DROs can also refer their clients for a full assessment of their work potential and can recommend a course of work-oriented rehabilitation at a government-sponsored Employment Rehabilitation Centre (ERC) and/or re-training through government-sponsored or other training schemes. Grants are made which cover training costs and a maintenance allowance for the worker and his family during the training period. Assistance is also, but not frequently, given to those who wish to set themselves up in business or in professional practice.

At its best, and particularly in periods of high employment, the service has achieved some notable successes which have demonstrated that it is possible with the co-operation of enlightened employers and concerned workmates to integrate into open employment people with a wide range of severe disabilities including many who would have been rejected for any kind of work until very recently.

Among the most difficult people to place are those recovering from psychiatric illnesses and those who, having once been labelled 'mentally subnormal' may have spent more than half a lifetime in institutions or hospitals, yet some from both these groups have been placed in full-time jobs at trade union rates of pay, are fully accepted by their colleagues, and occupy lodgings or their own homes in the community.

A small minority of rehabilitatees, which could almost certainly be much larger, actually improve their employment prospects by re-training for a new trade or profession after the onset of disability, but the occupational status of disabled people generally tends to be lower than that of the general population (see Table 10). Also, their choice of

TABLE 10

The occupational status of disabled men and women in employment compared with that of the general population. (Source: Harris et al. 1971. Table 13)

Occupational status	Disabled people	General population
	%	%
Employers and managers	11	12
Professional workers	2	3
Intermediate non-manual	5	6
Junior non-manual	20	22
Personal service	5	5
Foreman—manual	4	3
Skilled manual	21	23
Semi-skilled manual and agricultural	20	16
Unskilled manual	12	8
HM Forces	—	1
Other	—	1
	100	100

job tends to be restricted. They are frequently overlooked for promotion, and they tend to remain in the same job for longer than other workers since prospects of re-employment if they leave a post are lower.

The system described above is peculiar to the United Kingdom, but Vocational Rehabilitation Agencies in the USA offer a somewhat similar service and most advanced countries now legislate for the rehabilitation and re-employment of disabled workers. It is not possible here to detail the very varied patterns of legislation but it is probably a fair summary to say that in most countries a higher proportion of the onus in occupational rehabilitation is laid upon employers than in Britain. Each approach has its own advantages and disadvantages.

Where a high measure of responsibility is located at the place of work attention may be given to the more strictly environmental aspects of placement. In the UK an employer may occasionally receive a grant for the modification of, say, a machine—and this in turn may function as a trap restricting the worker's job mobility or chances of promotion. Little has been done to analyse occupational requirements and specific operations with a view to better matching of actual and potential skills to jobs, or the modification of job requirements.

We know of no project in this country to compare with the highly sophisticated system operated by Renault in France, as described by Dubot, Mirot and Salmon (1971). At the time of their report the total labour force at all Renault establishments amounted to 94 000, of whom some 11 000 (14 per cent) had some disability, and about 8 per cent of the total force was classified as 'seriously disabled'. After detailed job studies precise specifications of the physical, mental and sensory activities required in every job, and of the immediate working environment, are stored by computer. The capabilities of disabled workers are coded in complementary form by medical staff and the computer performs a preliminary matching which usually provides the applicant with a fair choice of available and reasonably suitable jobs. From that point, any necessary modification may be made in the preferred job specifications, and additional training may be given to the worker. Particular attention is given to rehabilitating workers into their former jobs where possible and job adaptations are common. Among examples quoted is the case of a welder wounded in the right forearm, affecting the median and cubital nerves. After intensive rehabilitation the worker resumed his job and thus retained his trade; the modification of the working position 'consisted simply of increasing the diameter of the stem of the welding torch'. A simple solution possibly, but likely to be achieved only when such matching objectives have been made explicit and a detailed analysis of both worker capability and basic job requirements have been made at the place of employment. As a result of their programme, Renault claim that 93 per cent of all rehabilitated workers are returned either to their former work (or the same job after modification) or to jobs with equivalent or higher status, and only 7 per cent (mainly people with chronic affections, generally alcoholism) have to change to jobs requiring lower qualifications.

Of course, the environmental problems of the employed disabled worker are not all encountered at his place of work. It is possible to be non-handicapped in the job itself but handicapped in other situations equally relevant to the successful retention of the ability to work. Johnson and Johnson (1973) in a study of paraplegics in Scotland noted some of these problems:

> As many paraplegics commented, the process of getting up and dressing in the morning was so exacting that . . . it was necessary to rise an hour or more before an able-bodied man. Travelling to work and manoeuvring a wheelchair into and out of a car added further physical strain even before the day began. One paraplegic relinquished his job because he found a 20 mile journey to work exhausting.

A great deal remains to be done to open up further employment opportunities for disabled adults and to ease the additional burdens that working may impose upon them.

Living in the community

1)   At Home
   Most people like to think that they have some choice in the matter of where they will make their home and with whom they will share it. In practice even many able-bodied people cannot exercise such a choice, but disability can impose additional restrictions on these freedoms. A disabled person may be unable to carry out such basic self-care tasks as washing, dressing or feeding himself, or using the toilet, or performing ordinary domestic tasks like preparing a meal, or answering the door or telephone (because he cannot hear the bell).
   Modern technology, however, can restore a remarkable measure of environmental control. There is now no technological reason why a deafened mother should not 'listen' for her baby's crying with the help of a flashing-light alarm while she watches a subtitled television programme on her own screen. The redesign of a home with widened doors, stair and bed hoists, adapted toilet facilities and kitchen fitments repositioned to bring everything within reach can make it possible for a chairbound housewife to look after herself and perform most of her domestic chores without human help. People capable only of using one finger or blowing lightly through a pneumatic tube can operate electronic selector mechanisms to choose television programmes, turn the pages of books, dial telephone numbers, open remote doors, set alarm systems in action, or, by the use of an adapted typewriter system linked to a visual display screen, write poetry or 'chat' with a friend. In principle all except a very small minority of disabled people could live in

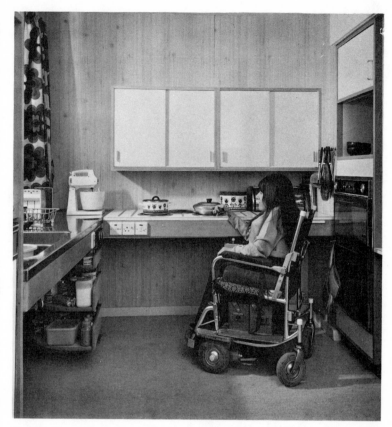

FIGURE 13 A young woman in her specially adapted kitchen at John Grooms
Princess Crescent Development. (Photograph: The Royal Association for Disability
and Rehabilitation)

their own homes if they so wished with support of the kind described
above plus some regular human help on hand when needed. Far too
many, however, still spend their days in hospital wards or in statutory
or voluntary residential homes. Although there has been in the last
thirty years a dramatic change for the better in the physical conditions
and in the quality of the care in the residences occupied by disabled
people, they are still even at their best institutions which segregate the
disabled from the mainstream of community living.

2) The world outside

For most people home is primarily a secure base, and much of our
living, by necessity and for pleasure, goes on outside it. Without

FIGURE 14   'Public lavatories were used by only 29 per cent.'—p. 85. (Photograph: The Royal Association for Disability and Rehabilitation)

opportunities to emerge it may seem little better than a prison. Younger adults in particular need to be out and about and those still living with parents usually want to move away and set up homes of their own. Selwyn Goldsmith, the British architect, whose *Designing for the Disabled* is a comprehensive manual of environmental adaptations, domestic and public, carried out a detailed study in 1964–8 of the entire wheelchair-using population (284 people) of one English city, Norwich (Goldsmith, 1976). His findings merit close attention. There is only room to look at some of them here.

Only a very small number of the people Goldsmith questioned (about 4 per cent) never left their homes. (The study was confined to wheelchair-users and there may of course have been many severely disabled people at home who did not use wheelchairs.) The facilities and buildings most frequently used outside the home were public parks (used by 60 per cent), stores, supermarkets or shops (by 46 per cent), cafés and restaurants and hospitals (by 40 per cent). Hairdressers, churches and chapels and clubs were all used by 20 per cent or more of the population, and hotels, post offices, public houses and cinemas by 10 per cent or more. Public lavatories were used by only 29 per cent, which might seem surprising were it not for the fact that they were also well at the head of the list of buildings regarded as inadequately accessible.

Goldsmith's findings on the age and sex distribution of wheelchair-users are interesting and are broadly compatible with those of other studies made in Britain. The mean age of his population was 60·4. Nearly two-thirds were women, with a mean age of 63·6. The mean age of the men was 54·6, but among all those aged less than 55 the number of men and women was almost equal (37:35); among those aged 75 and over the women outnumbered the men by more than 4 to 1. These findings reflect the tendency in the wider population to greater longevity in women and the increasing risk of disability as age increases.

Mobility, which correlated highly with youth, emerged as a very important factor in environmental usage. The small minority (1 in 9) who had vehicles they could drive independently made much more intensive and varied use of buildings outside their homes than all the others including the ambulant who used their chairs only occasionally. The 'independent chairbound' (i.e. those who habitually went out in their chairs unaccompanied) were also high users of the environment.

These groups included most of the people who had possessed their chairs for many years, often from childhood. It is this population of younger chair-using adults that in many countries has formed the spearhead of the movement for closer integration among disabled people in recent years. Such people are no longer willing to doze out their days in the wards of general hospitals and the community has responded in a variety of ways, some better than others, to their claims. Some of the earlier responses, like specially designed units for the younger chronically sick annexed to hospitals, and the Cheshire homes independent of hospitals but with nursing staff in attendance, were moves towards greater freedom and privacy but still in all essentials segregating institutions. Even the well-known Het Dorp village community in Holland which offers independent homes grouped into units, shopping and other small town facilities, and its own workshops for those who can work as well as clinical, therapy and support services for four hundred disabled people, does not appear to have resulted in close integration with the neighbouring able-bodied community. There can be no doubt however that it has brought a freer, more satisfying way of life to its inhabitants.

Perhaps the most sophisticated and influential project is the Fokus scheme in Sweden. In a modified form and on a much smaller scale it has been replicated in the Habinteg Housing Association scheme at Moira Close, Haringey, London. The Fokus Society began as a voluntary movement but proved so successful that it was taken over by the State. Its objectives are to provide the means for disabled people: (i) to live under the same conditions and with the same opportunities as the able-bodied; (ii) to live in security with access to reliable personal service; (iii) to live in a chosen geographical area; (iv) to have a choice of suitable occupation; (v) to enjoy stimulating and satisfying leisure activities.

There are at the time of writing thirteen Fokus units, ten of which are sited in the more densely populated central and southern parts of Sweden. Fokus flats, which may be for single people, two people, or larger families, are integrated into central housing areas. There may be anything between ten and thirty specially designed flats interspersed among flats for the general public. The buildings as well as the individual flats are so planned as to enable even the most severely disabled to maximize their capacities. There is easy, stepless access to all neighbourhood facilities including hobby and workrooms, restaurant, shopping centre, laundry, swimming pool, library, hospital or health centre, and, of course, car park. There is an around-the-clock staff which provides routine services as required and will also respond immediately to a signal system that will bring someone to any flat whenever a special need arises. All these services are included in the rental paid to the local authority. Many of the present occupants had previously lived as dependants with parents or other relatives, or in residential care. Again, the extent to which a programme of this kind can be achieved in practice in any given community depends upon the resources, material and human, that the community at its various levels is prepared to deploy.

3) Opening up the wider environment

The same argument applies to the removal of barriers to access, communication and travel in and between towns and cities. It may be argued that, in general, houses and public buildings and transport systems designed with disabled people in mind are more convenient and easier to live and work in for the rest of the population. Who regularly uses the stairs when there is a lift available? Who would refuse wide doors, plenty of circulation space and a really well-planned kitchen at home? Certainly few mothers with young children, older able-bodied people or furniture removals men. Can we not then aim to move steadily towards a total environment that would be fully accessible to and manageable by all able-bodied and disabled people alike?

The answer to this question cannot be a wholly unqualified 'yes'. More than immediate economic constraints are involved. There are, for

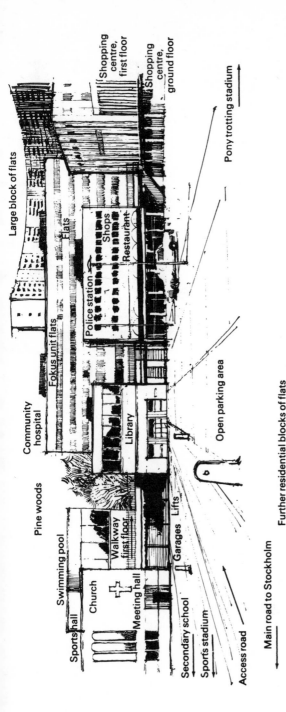

FIGURE 15   Fokus Housing Society, Sweden: impression of the Täby residential and shopping area. (Source: Brattgård, Sven-Olof. 1968. *Fokus—A Way to Form a Future*. Göteborg: Stiftelsen Fokus)

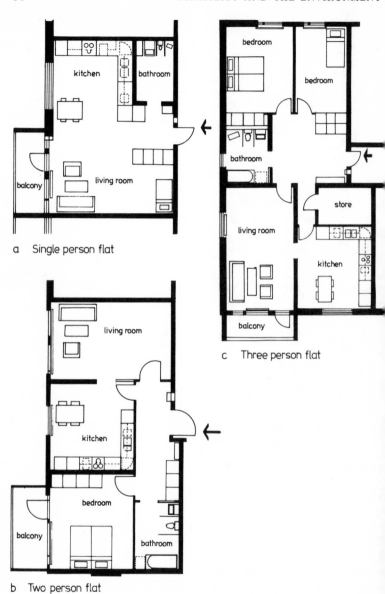

a   Single person flat

b   Two person flat

c   Three person flat

FIGURE 16   Fokus Housing Society: typical flat plans. (Source: Goldsmith, S. 1976. *Designing for the Disabled*. 3rd edn. London: RIBA Publications)

example, cultural and aesthetic considerations. No one would be prepared to demolish our heritage of magnificent pre-twentieth century domestic and public buildings because the steps make access by wheelchair difficult. We can only urge strongly that in the case of public buildings alternative means of access be provided where necessary.

Further, some real conflicts of interest exist, not only between the able-bodied and the disabled, but between people disabled in different ways. A kitchen designed with low working surfaces with chairbound housewives in mind would be uncomfortable for the average housewife and unworkable for an ambulant arthritic who found bending painful. The utopia we should plan for, then, is one in which the widest possible range of common needs is provided for, but where there is room for flexibility in catering for the needs of individuals. This can be costly, but some of the cost is directly recoverable by the community in the release of productive potential in handicapped people and indirectly in the greater convenience to all of an environment planned to minimize handicap. Furthermore, if measures such as those required by the Chronically Sick and Disabled Persons Act in Britain are scrupulously incorporated at the planning and design stage the costs are relatively light.

In recent years the community has been active at international as well as at national levels to improve the situation. For example, in 1972 the Council of Ministers of the Council of Europe adopted a resolution recommending that the governments represented should take 'all necessary measures ... to ensure that public buildings including privately owned buildings to which the public has access, should be constructed and fitted out in such a way as to make them more accessible to the physically handicapped'. Appended to the resolutions is a schedule of 'Measures to be taken' under three headings:

(i) *Measures common to all buildings and installations used by the public.* These include instructions (and in some cases specific measurements are given) for entrance at road level, wide communicating doors, straight staircases with broad steps (for people using crutches), handrails (both for support and for the guidance of blind people), lifts with suitably placed buttons and inter-phones, level entrances and non-slip covering for stairs, ramps and corridors, accessible toilets with handgrips on all floors, and suitably placed, accessible telephones.

(ii) *Specific measures for certain buildings.* The detailed recommendations under this heading cover post offices, theatres, cinemas, banks, stations, sports grounds, public baths and schools.

(iii) *Provision for parking.* In addition to special areas, with extra space for free movement when leaving or entering a vehicle, the recommendation requires the display of the appropriate international signs which should also be attached to handicapped persons' vehicles.

In this chapter we have offered evidence of an increasing awareness of the needs of adult disabled people and have provided examples of some outstanding initiatives towards meeting them. There are still however, very wide gaps between recommendation and general practice, and, in practice, between the best and the worst.

Age and Disability

What is ageing? Who is old?

When does a man or woman become old? And is old age a disability in its own right? The concepts of old age and ageing are not without ambiguity and call for some examination before we can attempt to answer these questions.

First, there is a subjective element in the way each man conceptualizes the stages of ageing which may be related to both the attitudes and practices of his immediate culture and to his own age at the time he attempts to answer the questions. Ethel Shanas (1970) wrote:

> 55 is considered the official beginning of old age in India, just as for most purposes, age 65 is the beginning of old age in the United States. Yet ... at the age of 70 most Americans continue to describe themselves as 'middle-aged', thus identifying with what they consider the mainstream of the American population. It is not until after they have reached the age of 75 that more than half of all Americans describe themselves as 'old' or 'elderly'.

And, from the opposite end of the life-span, the Beatles, acclaimed voice of youth in the 1960s, sang of 'When I'm sixty-four':

> I would be happy mending a fuse when your lights have gone.
> You could knit a sweater by the fireside,
> Sunday mornings go for a ride.
> Doing the garden, digging the weeds—who could ask for more?
> Will you still need me, will you still feed me,
> When I'm sixty-four?

Among older people those conceptualizations may also express unconscious denial of the approach of death. One conjectures that few of Shanas's 'middle-aged' seventy-year-olds seriously expect to live to be 140! Such attitudes are also, however, linked to the myths and stereotypes about old age that may be found in every culture.

Where these are unfavourable to the old they may function as a disabling factor in the ageing person's environment. In some civilizations old people have been regarded as the repositories of the wisdom of the tribe. Our own culture exhibits considerable ambivalence in its attitudes. The young may express the view that there can be nothing to live for after about forty, when life must surely become a burden to those who live on, and, by implication, to those who must work to maintain the old. The authority of older people who 'block promotion' or remain active in public affairs is resented. Ritual honours may be offered, from gold watches on retirement for the working man to peerages for politicians, sugar-coated hints that the time has come to 'move over'. The advertisements of some well-meaning charities do not help the image of the old, who are presented as cheerless, helpless and cold, worthy only of patronage. A positive aspect of this patronage, however, was reflected in a study of attitudes to the social services in Britain by Wedderburn (1967), who concluded: 'there was no doubt that it was the pensioners who commended most sympathy. Over half of all respondents thought that there were some social services on which the government should be spending more money and among these a large number wanted to see more money spent on widows or retirement pensioners in one form or another.' When we remember that we, too, will become old a certain sentimentality may soften the picture. A popular myth readily exploited by married sons and daughters in need of baby-sitters is that of a mystic bond between the old and the very young. This ambivalence on the part of the community may be reflected in a crisis of identity in some old people parallel to that experienced by some adolescents.

Second, there is the 'official beginning of old age', referred to by Shanas. Population statistics concerned with ageing assign each of us to an 'age group'. Social policy follows suit. The first payment of a retirement pension is linked to a date on a birth certificate, not (unless coincidentally) to an individual's reduced capacity to work, or any wish on his part to retire, or not to retire. From the date when official entitlement to a pension takes place most workers, whether compulsorily 'retired' by their employers or not, find themselves under steadily increasing pressure both from employers and from younger colleagues hungry for promotion.* In Britain receipt of a state pension does not necessarily require retirement, but most private occupational pension schemes do, and more than two-thirds of the male employee

---

* It is interesting here to compare the UK Census (1971) statistics of retirement for self-employed men with those men employed by others, keeping in mind that there may also be differences in job-satisfaction between the two groups. In the 65–9 age group 37·5 per cent of the self-employed were still working, and in the 70-and-over group 22·3 per cent. The proportions of those working but employed by others were 26·0 per cent and 11·0 per cent respectively.

population is now covered by such schemes. The clearest trend in retirement practice over the past few decades has been one towards compulsory retirement at or before sixty-five. Retirement, however, is almost invariably accompanied not only by changes in the patterns of daily living, but also by changes, usually for the worse, in social and economic status. These things are true for the non-employed wife of an employed man as well as for her husband. It seems that 'official old age' can also, at least in some cases, function as a handicapping factor in the environment.

Third, old age may be described, but not defined, in terms of biological processes associated with changes in functional capacity, but even biologists cannot remove all the ambiguities from the concept. Figure 1 in Chapter 2 summarized some observed effects of these processes. It is important to point out, however, that not only do the various functions deteriorate at different rates, but also there are wide differences in the rate at which they deteriorate in different individuals. We all know some spry and 'well-preserved' octogenarian, who appears to function generally better than many a man in his fifties. Biologists agree that a failure to renew certain cells in the body is characteristic of the ageing process, but in some organs this failure to renew begins very early in life while associated functions continue to develop and improve. Nevertheless, the later years of life are characterized by a general slowing down in physical activity, and in first the speed and then the quality of mental activity (as measured by intelligence tests), to a point where many of the daily tasks easily performed when younger cannot be undertaken at all. There is also an increased susceptibility to disease, including psychiatric disorders, and injury, and frequently a slower recovery rate. Until quite recently, old people who 'took to their beds' often believed that no treatment could ever get them on their feet again. Geriatricians, however, are now learning that old people's capacity for recovery is much greater than was once assumed. Nevertheless, the most determined and successful survivor will become progressively more generally frail with the passage of time and if no specific disease or injury fells him, will eventually sink into senescence, which Bromley (1966) describes as 'a general biological condition which predisposes the individual to die'. Below is his summarizing account of biological old age:

> Physical and mental diseases in old age are pathological conditions relatively distinct from, although superimposed upon and interacting with, the normal patterns of biological ageing and psychological change. But ageing can be regarded as an accumulation of pathological processes. Sensory and motor impairments—blindness and other visual defects,

deafness, paralyses, disablements—become more frequent
as age advances. Much depends upon one's standards of
comparison. An old person's blood pressure may be normal
relative to that of his age group, but abnormal relative to that
of a young healthy group. . . . A physical or mental condition
which is common to old people may be regarded as normal,
not pathological, whereas if it seriously disabled a few old
people it may be regarded as pathological. One might say,
paradoxically, that there are lots of normal old people, but no
healthy ones.

Causes of ageing

While the biological processes associated with ageing are still
imperfectly understood, there is no lack of theories as to its causes.
According to one, ageing is the *product* of the cumulative effects of
diseases and injuries acquired in the course of long interaction with a
hazardous environment. Another theory is that old age is genetically
determined, like childhood and puberty. While its onset may be
expedited by environmental stress, it is a stage in normal development
beginning before birth and ending in death. This view receives support
from population statistics, which show an increase in the number of
people surviving into their eighties and nineties in countries where
improved economic conditions have gone hand in hand with higher
standards of medical and social care, but offer no evidence that these
people are living longer than the lucky survivors of more hazardous
environments. The starting-point of this stage of development, some
writers suggest, should be taken as around the end of the normal period
of reproduction. It should be remembered, however, that this 'third age'
may well occupy more than one-third of any individual's life-span.

One implication of viewing old age as part of the normal developmental process should be to make us think again about the methods
used to evaluate function in older people. The common practice is to test
the old with instruments designed for the assessment of younger adults
and refer to differences found as 'decrements'. However, as long ago as
1958 Welford observed: 'Obviously there are ways in which a man or
woman matures and ripens into old age: the difficulty seems to be,
however, that these concern subtle aspects of human functioning, which
have not yet proved amenable to scientific investigation', and deplored
the failure of research to demonstrate them. There is some recent
evidence that even when traditional instruments are used old people may
actually perform better in some tasks than when they were younger. For
example, Savage *et al.* (1973) found significant rises in Performance IQ

on the well-known Wechsler Adult Intelligence Scale between the ages of seventy and seventy-six, although there was some fall in Verbal IQ.

In the field of education, Naylor and Harwood (1975) in Queensland, Australia, recently presented a dramatic challenge to the traditional view that old people are poor students. They gave instruction in German to eighty retired men and women with no previous knowledge of the language, whose ages ranged between sixty-three and ninety-one. They were not an intellectual elite. Their average IQ when measured on the Wechsler Adult Intelligence Scale was 102. Their educational background is described as 'decidedly meagre', more than half having had only primary education, and some having not completed even that. In occupational background, they ranged from waitresses and telephonists to civil servants, businessmen and teachers. After only three months' study, sixty-five students submitted themselves for an examination set at the level of the Australian Junior Examination taken by children after three years' study at secondary school. Forty-seven passed at or above that level and ten passed at the standard achieved by school pupils after two years. The authors report that their students refused to give up their studies at the end of the experiment and went on to further successes, some branching out into new fields of skills or knowledge, all taking up new social activities. It could be that with instruments designed to explore a wider range of functional abilities we might discover a great deal more unexpected potential in older people, to the eventual enrichment of their own lives and the community at large. One further point is worth making: while there are illnesses and accidents to which old people are more prone than younger people, there are none that occur only in old age. It follows then that except in cases of senescence, old age in itself should not be seen as necessarily a disability.

Ageing and disadvantage

The social survey of *Handicapped and Impaired in Great Britain* (Harris *et al.*, 1971) brought sharply into focus the relationship between ageing and disability in present-day society. It was estimated that 1 in 12 men and women aged 50–64 had some impairment, the proportion rising to just over 1 in 5 men and women aged 65–74, and about 1 in 3 men and 1 in 5 women aged 75 and over. Further, the likelihood of being included in one of the more severe categories of handicap (about 17 per cent of the total impaired) also increases with age. Table 11 summarizes the distribution of all impairment between age groups.

Before looking more closely at the relationship between ageing and certain environmental factors, however, it would be useful to remind

TABLE 11

The distribution of impairment between different age groups. Note that the age groupings are not at equal intervals. (Source: Harris *et al.* 1971. Table 1)

| Age group | Estimated no. in Gt. Britain | | | No. as % of all impaired |
	Men	Women	Men & Women	
16–29	50 000	39 000	89 000	2·9
30–49	197 000	170 000	366 000	11·9
50–64	401 000	433 000	833 000	27·1
65–74	356 000	599 000	915 000	29·8
75 & over	243 000	625 000	867 000	28·3
All ages	1 247 000	1 866 000	3 070 000	100·0

ourselves that in the more economically advanced countries today not only are many more people living longer lives than their grandparents did, but also the large majority of survivors do seem to retain their health and independence to the end or very near to it. Some remain active and creative well into their nineties. George Bernard Shaw (1856–1950) and Pablo Picasso (1881–1973) are two famous names that spring to mind, but an active old age is not the exclusive prerogative of genius. One of the authors of this book boasts an aunt, who, in her own words, 'didn't really begin to live' until an inheritance in her eighty-ninth year enabled her to set out on a trip round the world.

It is, however, unwise to overstress the 'achievement' of individuals in the light of incomplete knowledge both of individual backgrounds and of the factors favouring longevity in general. Nevertheless, the demographic evidence makes it clear that the environmental factors are of primary importance.

The association between survival after the age of about forty-five and economic and social advantage in the wealthier countries is made overwhelmingly clear in Figure 17. That the degree of environmental stress may also be differentially distributed according to economic advantage and working conditions within an 'advanced' country is suggested by the difference in life expectancy at birth between various socio-economic classes in France, according to Ledermann (1961) as follows:

Professionals	72–74 years
Office workers/clerks	68–70 years
Traders	65–67 years
Factory workers	63–65 years
Labourers	59–62 years
Miners	58–61 years

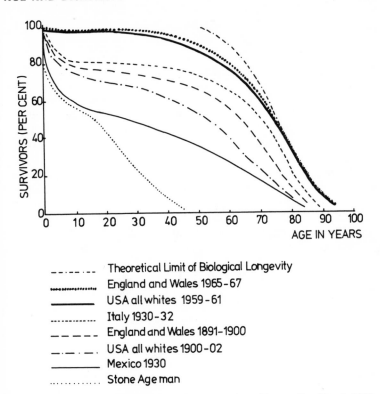

FIGURE 17   The mean age of death in seven populations. (Source: Comfort, A. 1973. Theories of ageing. In *Textbook of Geriatric Medicine and Gerontology*, ed. J. C. Brocklehurst. Edinburgh: Churchill)

According to Wisner (1975) 'marks' left by life constitute a major aspect of ageing, and he draws attention to the diversity of the risks to which individuals are differentially exposed—of an accidental, nutritional, infectious or toxic nature. Even the unborn child and the new-born infant are at risk under all these headings. Infectious illness in the mother may cause irreversible damage to the foetus or to the suckling infant. The drug Thalidomide is perhaps the best known example of a toxic substance which has resulted in permanent impairments before birth. Brain damage at birth may cause cerebral palsy, with effects that last a lifetime. Poor or faulty nutrition or in middle life the risks of injury and exposure to toxic substances at work vary between occupations, but tend in general to be higher among manual workers than in the professions. Certain heavily disabling diseases with effects that become more marked as the patient ages are specific to particular occupations, for example pneumoconiosis which reduces many retired miners to almost total dependency, and asbestosis affecting workers in the asbestos industry. Some industrial stresses take effect very gradually and it may be many years before the worker becomes fully aware himself of the 'mark'. Wisner quotes a survey by Ho and Quinot (1974) of workers exposed for thirty years to two levels of noise. At 90 dB, 35 per cent of the workers had a hearing loss of 25 dB (definition of deafness by ISO recommendations). At 100 dB (very frequent in workshops) the figure rose to 70 per cent. Another study quoted by Wisner is that of Clement, Cendron and Housset (1968) who investigated two groups of factory workers, one of average age 34 and the other of average age 54, both employed in a large automobile enterprise in the Paris region, and compared them with groups from other social classes (e.g. teachers). They found deterioration characteristic of ageing was much more rapid among the factory workers: systolic blood pressure was higher, resting cardiac rhythm quicker, physical strength weaker, and deterioration in intellectual ability and memory was more marked. Also, the frequency of cardio-vascular complaints and the use of sleeping tablets was much higher. Wisner also points out that the long-term effects of infectious diseases and even minor injuries may be compounded by neglect or poor medical services.

Ageing and retirement

By the time a person comes to the 'official age' for retirement, then, both biological and environmental processes will have contributed to the determination of the pattern of his life to come. These factors of course interact so closely that it is not possible to make any precise assessment of their relative contribution in any individual case. But retirement itself, as we have seen, is not a wholly voluntary act, and involuntary action is action undertaken under environmental pressure. Even when a worker goes willingly into retirement, however, he may be unprepared for the changes that it will bring about in his life. It may or may not be true (and it has not been proved either way) that, as Irene Gore has suggested, 'retirement probably kills more people, especially men, than do all the hazards, strains and stresses of working'. The frequently quoted death rate from suicide in England and Wales, however, is probably not irrelevant. Among women, the rate rises from 17 per 100 000 persons aged 45–64 to 19 aged 65–74 and drops to 13 aged 75 and over, while the comparable figures for men are 24, 33 and 39 respectively. Far fewer women than men, of course, are fully employed outside their own homes in middle and later life, and most of those who have been employed probably enjoy some continuity of role in the home well into old age.

Suicide, however, is an extreme and comparatively rare reaction to stress and in some cases mental illness. What are the particular environmental hazards associated with retirement in so far as these can be separated from the other effects of ageing? They are:

1. A change (usually quite sudden) in social roles, status and range of contacts.
2. A change (commonly for the worse) in economic status.
3. Exposure (particularly in those who live alone) to a variety of health risks often associated with unsuitable housing, reduced capacity for self-care, malnutrition, etc.

All these factors of course, interact with one another. It should also be stressed here that among those who experience all or some of these effects in some degree many (perhaps the majority) adapt well, live comfortably in somewhat reduced circumstances, find new, if more restricted, roles and interests, and may live for many years without any major illnesses or accidents.

Retirement in the modern sense of the word, the 'pensioning-off' of the mass of the working population, fit or unfit for further work, at an age determined by state, employer or insurance scheme, has developed differently in different countries, but in all it has a fairly short history. The demands of workers' organizations for a pension, as of right, in old age 'to supplement savings' have been conceded slowly. The principle of a pension as an *alternative* to savings is not even now accepted by all governments, and the price of acceptance to the workers, i.e. virtually enforced disengagement from the mainstream of social and economic life, is only now beginning to be understood. Retirement for most men implies the acceptance of a change of role. The respected member of a working team takes on overnight a new label. Whether the label reads 'old age pensioner' or 'senior citizen' makes very little difference in practice. His skills of a lifetime are no longer wanted; his habits must change as every day becomes a Sunday.

At home, from being a breadwinner and head of the family, he becomes an obstacle in his wife's familiar routine. When he tries to rejoin the social life of old workmates he finds himself an outsider, fit company only for other old men. Not surprisingly, a movement has developed in many places for education for retirement, for the cultivation of new interests and hobbies, but many men still find it difficult to accept the sudden change of role that retirement thrusts upon them.

For women the position is rather different. Only a minority in even the advanced industrialized countries continuously follow a career outside the home to an official retirement age. For those who do, retirement may present challenges—and problems—similar to those facing men. Many women, however, still retire permanently from paid employment when they marry or have their first child. Even those who return to work at some time during marriage have experience of a second domestic career to which they can return. However, there is one crisis of later life that is more likely to affect women than men: the crisis of widowhood. Three or four in every ten people over sixty-five in Britain are single or widowed women and the proportion is greater in the later years, because of the greater average longevity of women. For both sexes, family, friendship and neighbourhood ties tend to become increasingly important in later life, both as a means to social participation and as a protective network against failing health or accident. Where these are lacking the 'disengagement' of retirement or widowhood may be the prelude to social isolation, inactivity, and depression, and may put older people physically at risk with ill health or decreasing capacity to cope.

In the majority of cases retirement is accompanied by a reduction in income, which does not mean of course that all old people experience poverty. However, for some retirement does mean relative and sometimes absolute poverty, and this has been particularly true in recent years since savings and private pension-schemes are rarely inflation-proof. In most economically advanced countries, it is true, state provision for the elderly has improved in post-war years, but often slowly. In Britain, for example, the state retirement pension for a married couple as a percentage of average male earnings rose slowly from about 31 per cent in 1948 to about 34 per cent in 1967. In November 1975 this pension was increased to £21.20, which represented approximately 35 per cent of average earnings, and in November 1976 it increased to £24.50, which is about 36 per cent of average earnings for the preceding year. For those in greatest need supplementary assistance in cash, specific rebates and benefits in kind are obtainable (see Chapter 7, page 109), but not always obtained because of either ignorance, or reluctance to apply—or, sometimes, because of reluctance to give on the part of those responsible for administering assistance. Among the effects of an inadequate income may be unsuitable housing conditions, restricted mobility, under-nourishment, coldness in winter and (for some the most painful of all) an unmerited sense of worthlessness.

Unsuitable housing is a particular hazard for the old. Ageing people are often reluctant to leave a familiar neighbourhood but houses age, like people; the neighbourhood itself becomes 'run down' and younger neighbours, including the children and grandchildren of the old person, move away leaving behind them what has been called a 'geriatric ghetto'. The alternative of a dream bungalow by the sea for a retired couple can turn, when one partner dies, into a nightmare among strangers for the survivor. There is no single, simple solution to suit all cases. Certainly, the degree of personal disability is not the only criterion to be considered if we try to decide which individuals are most likely to be 'at risk'. The old person who is fortunate enough to be a welcome member of an extended family home may never have need of help from outside, but this is not a solution that is possible for or wanted by the majority of old people. For those who can live independently, regular contacts with children, grandchildren and friends can provide both personal satisfaction and some protection against the hazards associated with ageing, but the responsibility for providing substitute networks rests with the social services in those cases where old and frail people have inadequate contact with neighbourhood communities. Only a fully aware and caring community at all levels can protect the normally ageing from becoming the old and disabled before their time.

The breakdown of independent functioning

While we must expect that a larger proportion of older people may become impaired this obviously offers no valid reason for denying any individual, whatever his chronological age, the kind of rehabilitative and support services that have been discussed in earlier chapters. For some people, however, a point may eventually be reached when the individual is no longer able to choose his own mode of environmental control. His major decisions have to be taken by somebody else. The conditions that precipitate such breakdowns in the independent functioning of ageing people are multifarious: illnesses, accidents, increasing severity of long-standing disabilities, changes in the immediate social environment, or the accumulation of small difficulties to the point where the ability to cope with daily living becomes impossible. It should be the objective of those concerned with the welfare of old people to prevent that point arriving, if possible, and, if it should arrive, to attempt to restore the decision-making to its rightful owner. This is of course a counsel of perfection. For many old people even the best rehabilitation programme will leave them with greatly reduced options. Following a period in hospital an elderly person's functional capacities, physical and mental, may be so reduced that he cannot be expected to resume his old pattern of living. Those caring for him must make full assessments of his physical, functional, psychological and social prospects and give him not only the best treatment but also responsible advice. They must also take account of the needs of his immediate family, if he has been living with them. While most people, including most old people, would agree that care 'at home' is preferable to care 'in a home' not every family can stand up to the stress of caring for a sick elderly relative. There is no social gain in 'solving' the problems of a disabled and isolated old person by creating a disabled and isolated family. A caring society can provide a wide range of options between the extremes of enforced institutionalization 'for the patient's own good' and an unplanned return to the conditions that precipitated the breakdown. The Fokus scheme discussed in Chapter 5 provides one model, as suitable for some older disabled people as for those in middle life. 'Granny apartments' attached to family homes enable some old people to retain independence with the comfort and security of their relations close at hand. Organized neighbourhood support, including nursing services, help with the housework and alarm systems for calling neighbours in emergencies, can make it possible for people who live alone to remain in their own homes if they wish. The segregation of large groups of old people into residential homes or hospital wards while they are still capable of sustaining an individual life-style in the community is now rejected by all enlightened gerentologists, as well as by most old people. There will always, however, be some old people heavily disabled, terminally ill, mentally confused or very tired, who want only to be allowed to rest awhile without pain before the end. This too is a 'decision' that those who have assumed responsibility for another person must be prepared to honour.

7

Looking Ahead

Throughout this book we have tried to summarize the needs and, as we see them, the legitimate demands of impaired people to choose for themselves an individual life-style in the community that compares in quality with that of unimpaired people. We have analysed the stresses to which they are exposed in an environment that has been adapted by many successive generations of the unimpaired to give priority to their own needs. We have also recognized the very considerable advances made in recent years in the field of rehabilitation which focuses upon the impaired individual and aims to restore as much as possible of his physical, mental and social capacity by medical means, appliances and aids, and by re-training in some of the basic skills needed for self-care and gainful employment. We have recognized too a growing awareness of the need to make changes in the wider environment reflected in legislation concerned with the education, employment, housing, mobility and economic status of disabled people. These advances, however, should not blind us to the fact that much remains to be done if the objectives we have outlined above are to be achieved, and we have also made clear our view that the most sophisticated professional rehabilitation service cannot achieve them unless the community at large accepts and supports the claim of impaired people to full and equal citizenship, including the right of participation in all the decision-making processes that may affect them in their personal or in their public lives.

Public attitudes and action

In writing this book we had a clearly avowed practical aim: by presenting the facts as we see them we hoped to stimulate change. We have said in several places that action depends in the final analysis upon the attitudes of individuals, both disabled and non-disabled. Among the environmental factors that stand in the way of change, however, perhaps the most insidious, if least easily defined, are many commonly held but not always openly expressed attitudes towards disability. Not all prejudiced behaviour stems from consciously held hostility. Ignorance which leads to blind stigmatizing, fear, and the paternalistic benevolence which 'knows what is best for others' may all play some part in unfavourable attitude formation.

The concept of 'attitude' has a long history in psychology. A brief definition by Rokeach (1968) summarizes a number of approaches: 'An attitude is a relatively enduring organization of beliefs around an object or situation predisposing one to respond in some preferential manner.' It is impossible to review fully here the literature on attitudes to disabled people, but there is general agreement upon two points:

1. that attitudes to visibly disabled people commonly lead to their devaluation;
2. that attitudes vary towards different disabilities, some being viewed less unfavourably than others. The hierarchy of unfavourability has varied at different times and in different cultures but in present-day western society, for example, blind people generally are less devalued than people with facial disfigurement, communication difficulties, bizarre movements or epilepsy.

Attitudes of course vary also from one individual to another within a community. Goffman (1968) writes: 'In most cases . . . [the stigmatized person] will find that there are sympathetic others who are ready to adopt his standpoint in the world and to share with him the feeling that he is human and "essentially" normal in spite of appearances and in spite of his own self-doubts.' He describes two such categories: (i) those who share his stigma, whom Goffman calls 'the own' and (ii) those others who through family, friendship, professional or work situation, or even accident have developed a special understanding and sympathetic relationship with the stigmatized group. These Goffman calls 'the wise'. The spearhead of community action is often an alliance between 'own' and 'wise'. Also, a considerable group in many communities may consist of people who, having no immediate contact with the stigmatized, may have only weak or inconsistent attitudes towards them. Or attitudes may be selective, 'wise' in relation to one group of disabled people and hostile towards another.

There is also some research which indicates that attitudes as measured by the traditional questionnaire type of test are not always reliable predictors of behaviour. La Piere (1934) and Kutner et al. (1952), for example, found marked discrepancies among restaurant and hotel owners in America between their verbal expression of discrimination towards Chinese and Negroes via letter or telephone and their comparatively non-discriminatory behaviour in the face-to-face situation. Rokeach points out that people are not motivated by a single attitude and argues that we have attitudes towards 'situations' (such as, in the quoted example, the right way to run a restaurant) as well as towards 'objects' (including stigmatized minorities). Since an attitude-object must always be encountered within some situation about which we also have an attitude, he suggests, a minimum condition for social behaviour is the activation of at least two interacting attitudes, one concerning the attitude-object and the other concerning the situation.

It is, then, difficult to make general statements about how 'community attitudes' may or may not be translated into action likely to produce large-scale environmental changes. It seems however a tenable hypothesis that changes which make it possible for disabled people to appear more frequently in 'normal' situations may of themselves tend to produce attitude changes in favour of yet further environmental change. Initiatives taken at any level of the community should have a cumulative effect.

The implications of change

Underlying the case for environmental change is the assumption that a fairer, more humane community is a better community for all. But it would be hypocritical to pretend that effects of changes in favour of any particular section of the community are always immediately experienced as beneficial by others. Particularly in periods of low economic growth, any redistribution of resources inevitably implies some robbing of Peter in the interests of Paul. Change, however, demands the making of many often difficult and complex decisions, individually and collectively, at all levels of the community. We have chosen to discuss this problem here in terms of income needs, since all of us recognize in our own lives that spending power is the most important single ingredient in personal autonomy. It seems to us that the important thing is to realize the need for formulating priorities and for decisions and action based upon thoughtful consideration of the available information as well as of the views of others.

The cost

Even when the disability is one where legal redress has been possible the State still retains a major interest in and bears the major part of the cost of disability. Some idea of the relative costs is shown in Table 12, and even though 'accidental' injuries account for only a small proportion of the total number of disabled people, their estimated costs in compensation or benefit were £146 million, of which less than half came from state or personal insurance. This data was collected as a

TABLE 12

Estimated compensation for personal injury in 1970. (Source: Doherty, N. A. & Lees D. S. 1974. Damages for personal injury—some economic issues. In *Impairment Disability and Handicap*, ed. D. Lees & S. Shaw, p. 68. London: Heinemann)

Source	Road Accidents £m	Industrial Accidents £m	Other £m	Total £m
(1) Social Security Benefit				
Sickness	7·3	not applicable		
Death	4·9	,,	} 38·7	
Supplementary	0·6	,,		
Industrial Injury	not available	33·4	not applicable	
Industrial Disablement	,,	60·6	,,	
Industrial Death	,,	8·5	,,	
Total	12·8[1]	102·5[2]	38·7	154·(
(2) Tort	50·0	27·5[3]	14·0	91·.
(3) Sick pay	2·7	18·5	28·2	49·.
(4) Personal Insurance	11·6	2·2	21·8	35·(
(5) National Health	11·6	23·0	50·9	85·.
(6) Totals	88·7	173·7	153·6	416·(

[1] This figure will probably underestimate the total social security payments to roa˙ accident victims. Some accident victims will have qualified for the industrial benefits ˙ their accidents occurred out of and in the course of their employment.

[2] Payment for prescribed diseases is included but accounts for a relatively smal˙ proportion of the total.

[3] These figures differ slightly from those presented by us in D. S. Lees and N. Doherty 'Compensation for Personal Injury', *Lloyds Bank Review*, April 1973. The reason i˙ that more complete records of company returns to the Department of Trade an˙ Industry and other data are now available.

special exercise in 1970 and, therefore, the monetary values have been˙ overtaken by inflation (approximately doubled). Nevertheless in relative terms there is unlikely to have been any change—state or persona˙ insurance still does not compensate for disability.

The poverty of the disabled is confirmed by a special investigation conducted in Britain under the auspices of the General Household Survey, a continuing government-sponsored investigation of various aspects of the population. A report in 1973 was produced of a specia˙ study in 1971 of the chronic sick. It showed that:

> The head of the household containing chronic sick people was most likely to be amongst those with a weekly income of less than £16 a week and was very heavily over-represented amongst those whose weekly income was £10 or under. The

difference between the housing conditions of the chronic sick
and the non-chronic sick was less marked than the differences
in income level. A higher proportion of people in rented than
in owner-occupied accommodation were chronic sick,
particularly in the private unfurnished sector. Chronic
sickness was more common amongst people living in housing
built before 1919, in accommodation without central heating,
without a fixed bath and without a lavatory; and in
accommodation with a lavatory it was most common where
the entrance to the lavatory was outside the building.

. similar study at about the same time in the USA gave comparable
esults. It found that half the disabled had income below the poverty
ne, and the more severe the disablement the lower the income. It
btained parallel findings to those of the GHS on home ownership,
wnership of consumer durables, financial assets, and membership of
nancial plans such as occupational pension schemes.
  The problem begins with employment. In response to a
arliamentary question on 30 January 1973, the then Secretary of State
or employment in the UK produced a table which shows that
nemployment of the registered disabled consistently runs at a rate
hree times higher than that of the general population.
  This problem is discussed more fully in a memorandum published by
he Association of Disabled Professionals (Large, 1973) in response to
he consultative document of the Department of Employment on the
quota scheme' for disabled people (Department of Employment, 1973).
The memorandum points out that there is an estimated pool of 625,000
eople who could be registered under the quota scheme, and that this
umber is higher than the numbers of employed (500,000) and
nemployed (72,000) disabled people on the register at the time of
ublication. It is clear from such data that we are not planning for a
mall group of disabled people. Rather we are planning for a group of
eople for whom 'no precise estimate is possible, but it would be unwise
o assume that the number would be other than quite a large one'—a
roup of people who have as much right to expect society to adjust to
hem as society has to expect them to adjust to it.
  Unemployment is only the start of the problem. When a disabled per-
on is successful in obtaining a job, as we saw in Chapter 5, he is likely to
e employed below his capability when compared with his peers who are
ortunate enough not to be disabled. We see this clearly in the income
tatistics. The point is also illustrated in the definitive National Census
f the Deaf conducted in the USA in 1970. Schein and Delk (1974)
eport data confirming that a group of disabled people who are
elatively better placed in employment prospects than many of their

peers are still discriminated against economically. They also report on
the present occupations of this group and conclude:

> In terms of occupations, deaf workers are far behind in
> professional, technical, clerical, sales and service
> positions—the four fastest growing categories. Deaf workers
> have higher proportions than they should have in the
> craftsmen and operator categories, if they are to maintain
> their present and anticipated share of the labour force. Deaf
> persons are also grossly underrepresented among the
> managers, officials and proprietors, and greatly over-
> represented among labourers, farm and nonfarm-workers
> combined.

Income maintenance

Britain has a variety of State cash benefits designed to provide
income for disabled people and the families of disabled children. An
excellent guide through this rather complex maze is provided in the
Disability Rights Handbook for 1977 (Disability Alliance, 1976). In
assessing the merit of such provision we have to take account of the fact
that there is no wholly satisfactory method of defining a minimum
standard of living or, indeed, way of life. For this reason there can be no
absolute measure of poverty, although State supplementary benefits are
designed to provide what is judged to be a socially acceptable minimum
standard of support adequate to meet everyday basic requirements.
Whether they do so or not is a matter of considerable controversy, and
whatever support is provided it is unlikely that a consensus will ever be
reached. Opinions about the extent to which resources are redistributed
in favour of those least well provided for is a matter of political opinion,
social values and life experiences. We referred in the first chapter to the
increased political awareness of disabled people, and 'lobbying' by
groups representing them has increased considerably in recent years. In
the field of income maintenance one such group in Great Britain has
been the Disability Alliance* who believe along with many others that
more needs to be done. They have concluded that:

> If we concentrate attention therefore on poverty as defined by
> the State there is evidence both that a substantial section of
> the disabled legally entitled to supplementary benefit live in
> poverty, and that the scheme is currently failing to meet their

---

* The Disability Alliance is a coalition research and pressure group formed in 1974
with the support of more than twenty separate organizations of and for disabled people.

poverty even when they are receiving benefits. And it must be
remembered that there are other groups of the disabled living
in poverty who are not covered by the scope of the supplementary benefit scheme—many handicapped children,
disabled housewives and disabled men and women who are in
low-paid employment.*

The agreement amongst those concerned with disability extends to
seeing the need for a more effective and administratively simpler scheme
for income maintenance for disabled people, although better
opportunities for education, training and employment are of equal if not
greater concern. Those who propose such schemes feel that until they
are available disabled people will gravitate to the poorer segments of our
society. They often fail to realize that the cost will be high, and the
community must decide if and when it is prepared to meet this cost.
It is not that nebulous entity, 'the State', that will provide the
resources—they will only come from greater effort and sacrifice by the
rest of the community, sacrifice of personal income, or other public
services, or more probably both. One scheme has been suggested by
Disability Alliance, and whilst it is possible to argue the merits or
otherwise of details it is fair to say that it has identified those crucial
aspects of disability which need to be taken into account when
considering the form of any benefit for disabled people. Disability
Alliance feel that any composite scheme must take into account long-
term disability from which total or partial recovery is possible, as well as
permanent partial or total disability, and must also make special
provision for the often major expenses which have to be met by disabled
people as a direct result of their disability. They also suggest that any
benefits available under such a scheme must be based on the disability
itself, and not on the previous employment history or on the cause of
disablement as is the case with many existing benefits in most countries.
Legislatively and administratively implementing a scheme such as that
of Disability Alliance is extremely complex, but as long as an
industrially disabled worker may be reasonably cushioned from the
financial effects of disability but a congenitally handicapped housewife
is not, we have a society in which the circumstances of the injury do
more to determine benefit than the nature of the disability. Although
this is the present state of affairs in Great Britain and many other
countries, a start has been made in Britain by establishing not only a
non-contributory invalidity benefit for housewives, but other non-
contributory benefits such as the constant-attendance allowance for
parents of handicapped children and the mobility allowance for

* Since the publication of this statement disabled housewives in the UK who meet
certain specified criteria became eligible (in 1977) for a disability pension.

disabled adults and children. Similarly, 'no fault' insurance schemes in the USA are also beginning to remove the discrimination that exists between road accident victims—those whose accident was the 'fault' (by legal definition) of an appropriately insured driver or pedestrian, and those whose accident did not take place in such circumstances.

The role of the community

It should go without saying, of course, that environmental changes take place continuously irrespective of any formal planning at national or local government levels. Indeed only a hundred years ago people would have considered it blasphemous to imagine that humans might presume to intervene in the design of their total environment. Today the man in the street tends to believe that between them politicians and scientists can and should reshape the universe immediately to bring it in line with the leading article of his morning newspaper. Any planned change, too, may have wide-ranging unplanned effects. Nevertheless, the planning of change, formal and informal, collectively and individually, does take place, and in a variety of ways we are all able to influence its direction.

At several points in this book we have suggested that the community should take responsibility for initiating change. This concept is a complex one to which we cannot do justice fully in a short book, but we cannot avoid a discussion of its implications in the context of disability. The word 'community' is one of the most overworked nouns in the English language. It appears in the literature of sociology, social behaviour and social work with nearly as many variations of meaning as it receives mention. In popular writings it commonly has emotive overtones. It refers to 'our county', 'our town,' 'our neighbourhood' or 'our way of life' and implies strong common values, feelings and bonds, which rarely in practice correspond to the realities of existence in modern, urbanized societies as revealed by objective studies of attitudes and social behaviour.

Bayley (1973), who made a study of patterns of the community care of mentally handicapped adults in Britain, maintains that 'a sense of belonging, locality and the existence of reciprocal social relationships' are the three most generally accepted elements encompassed by the concept of 'community', and suggests that it is meaningful to talk about three levels of community based upon geographical locality and population size. In the context of community care for the handicapped these, he holds, can be crudely equated with three administrative levels:

1. At the most general level the community is the nation, i.e. the total population seen as a complete social, economic and political

system, and equated at the administrative level with 'central government'. Government determines the pattern of care through legislation and is also responsible for the diversion of resources to make changes effective. In a democracy, the 'governed' play their part in directing policy not only through the ballot box but also through a network of consultative bodies and pressure groups, through press and media, and as individuals making their views and feelings felt in a hundred different ways.

2. Second, there is the village, town or county level of community. Bayley argues, however, that although historically the local integrated community, distinguished by an awareness of separate identity, communal solidarity and mutual support, was once a social reality it is in modern technological societies rapidly becoming obsolescent. Nevertheless, local authorities, controlled by the elected representatives of the population, have administrative responsibility for the well-being of the people within their designated boundaries.

3. Third, Bayley identifies a small-scale level of intimate face-to-face relationships, of social networks of kin, friends and neighbours, which can still be recognized as meeting the three basic criteria. Although he has some difficulty in defining an 'administrative level' to correspond with the face-to-face community he nevertheless regards the latter as the basis upon which depends all community care of the mentally handicapped (and we would say the true integration of disabled people generally) at the larger-scale levels. He illustrates this by reference to the National Health Service in Britain. It is not, he says, 'based on the general practitioners, vital though they are, but the mothers who nurse their children through the common infectious diseases, the relatives who help during childbirth, the neighbours who lend a hand when a mother is ill at home ... The National Health Service does not replace care by the community at this level but it builds on it and strengthens it'. Even when under stress the small-scale community continues to contain and sustain its 'own', with some support from the social services. It does emerge clearly, however, from the report of his detailed study of severely mentally handicapped adults living in their own homes in one large industrial city, that when the person in need of care is a heavily handicapped adult the stress imposed upon the family and particularly upon the individual doing the lion's share of the caring—most commonly a mother or other female relative—may be very severe indeed, and may appear as a life sentence, albeit ungrudgingly accepted. Support from kin and neighbourhood may be slight and only intermittent.

Bayley also draws attention to another important usage of the term, *the community of common interests*, and he quotes the example of 'a community of scholars'. This usage corresponds in many ways to the concept of a subculture, but does not carry the rather patronizing overtones associated with the latter term. In the context of disability, common-interest communities which may extend beyond narrow locality boundaries frequently exist among disabled people. The 'deaf world' for example is truly international and a deaf adult without speech can often communicate more freely with another deaf person from a different country than with a hearing person from his own. It is important to emphasize that such common-interest communities are not inimical to the idea of full integration. We would not expect a person of strong but minority religious views to give up his links with those who share his interests and values as the price of full and equal membership of the wider community. Integration does however require us to accept the social institutions of minority cultures and welcome them for whatever contribution they can make to the richness and variety of the life of the community at large.

Another important 'community of common interests' is the voluntary organization. Today nearly every recognized disabling condition has its own 'society', often with international connections. The older and larger societies, notably those concerned with the welfare of blind people, were in most cases founded by small groups of philanthropically minded people to fulfil fairly limited charitable objectives, but today they control quite considerable funds and have diversified their activities into such fields as education, careers training, residential care and research, and have a powerful influence on the policies of government and the practices of the statutory services. Their role in recent years has been repeatedly submitted to re-examination, partly as a result of their own past successes. The provision of day-to-day services for handicapped people has increasingly been taken over by statutory authorities financed through taxation and manned by professionals. During the same period there has been a steady growth of organizations and pressure groups composed of disabled people themselves and/or their families, whose values have not always coincided with the values of the older charities. Hopefully the day is in sight, in the wake of new thinking this changed situation has produced, when the many common-interest communities concerned specifically with disability will close ranks and speak with one voice.

Lastly, in the context of common-interest communities it is worth while considering the many professional and para-professional groups who operate the services offered to disabled people. They have much in common with each other. They are, and they feel themselves to be, the experts, the trained possessors of specialist skills. Their knowledge and value systems, the latter often embedded in formal codes of ethics, they in turn pass on to succeeding generations of experts through their control of professional education. They are also the servants of the taxpayers who provide their salaries, and of their individual clients whose need for a service keeps them in employment. Beyond that point it would, however, be rash to think of 'the professionals' as a single cohesive common-interest community. They subdivide into a large and ever-increasing number of specialized groups. It is no exaggeration to suggest that a child born with a disability may in his lifetime receive treatment or advice from people trained in thirty different disciplines, from surgeons, physicians, and specialists in a range of different therapeutic treatments, aid technicians, hospital and community nurses and social workers, psychologists, teachers, special skills trainers, employment experts and many more. Each group has its own self-delineated area of expertise, which it may guard jealousy both from the laity and from other professional groups. Indeed, they may even have difficulty at times in communicating across subgroup barriers, for out of a common dictionary they have developed some very uncommon language usages. Thus, to a psychologist 'conditioning' is a dispassionate term used to describe the way learning takes place when a response is reinforced by an environmental change experienced by the respondent as either satisfying or unpleasant. To some social workers it is a highly emotive expression evocative of manipulative practices imposed against their will upon helpless victims of unscrupulous therapists. The fact that the groupings themselves frequently stand in hierarchical relationship to one another also operates against the cohesiveness of the wider common-interest community of professional workers.

Individual responsibility

An important thing to keep in mind when we think of 'the community' as taking responsibility or initiating action is that at all levels the community is composed of individuals. To act as a member of a community implies finding common ground, sinking differences and acting together in a common cause. This has obvious advantages. Two heads, we are told, are better than one, and many hands make light work, although it is questionable whether the rules of simple arithmetic continue to apply as numbers increase. Unless each individual recognizes his own responsibility a point is rapidly reached where it becomes easy to 'leave things to others' or, worse still, to 'leave them to the experts'. The danger exists at all levels of the community. Local authorities have neglected possible initiatives while 'waiting for a lead' from central government—which in turn may 'wait' until public pressure forces action. Also, close community links, particularly of the interest-community type, can blind members to the needs of wider communities. It is easy, for example, for a professional grouping to perceive itself as the unique custodian of a body of knowledge and expertise which it would be dangerous to share with other professionals and even more dangerous to pass on to the public. Quite arbitrary lines may be drawn between what a trained nurse may do and what is the proper sphere of action for a social worker. A handicapped client, however, is not divided into a number of compartments each needing a separate service. He is a whole person and his needs are continuous, and perhaps the most important of them is that those who come into contact with him should treat him as a person, should trust him and should trust each other. We can usually learn more about handicap and how it can be reduced by talking to handicapped people and their families than by reading about specific disabilities in a textbook. Similarly, the good professional should, we believe, be willing to share as much as he can of his professional expertise with other professionals and with members of the wider community, impaired and unimpaired. It is unlikely (and probably undesirable) that a position will ever be reached when all the needs of disabled people will be met by trained professional workers. Certainly for a long time to come neighbourhood communities will continue to be an important service resource for the disabled—and in this field even a little learning is much less dangerous than blind ignorance.

In discussing social attitudes towards the handicapped, we must not allow society to become the scapegoat for our own individual problems. Whether a member of the general public or a professional working with disabled and handicapped people, we have to change our values and see working with them as a partnership. We have to get away from the motives of self-satisfaction which stress *helping* those less fortunate than ourselves. We cannot help the disabled but we can provide them with opportunities to help themselves and we can interact with them to enable both the disabled and the 'non-disabled' person to grow together. As a doctor undertaking an operation, a teacher teaching the child in basic academic skills, a rehabilitation counsellor or social worker attempting to provide occupational skills or opportunities, or as a neighbour guiding a blind person across the road, we have to see our work as a privilege that the disabled person confers on us rather than as something that reflects our own humanity towards our fellow man. It is easy to be 'kind' to someone whose power to resist patronage is small. A true democracy has no room for patronage: it depends upon respect by all for the essential humanity in every other member.

In practice, of course, no community group operates at any time entirely independently of all others, and individuals may be continuously acting and exerting influence, whether by intention, habit or default, at a variety of levels and through several different group alignments. To be effective an individual also needs to be clear in his own mind about his attitudes, priorities and scope of influence. Innumerable individual decisions, great and small, each depending upon the evaluation of particular circumstances and options, will determine the direction of progress. In this book, we have not tried to pre-empt these decisions, but we hope we have made some of them less difficult by presenting some of the facts and problems as fairly as we can.

Bibliography

Chapter 1

Agerholm, M. 1975. Handicaps and the handicapped: a nomenclature and classification of intrinsic handicaps. *Royal Society of Health Journal*, **95**, 3–8.

Department of Employment. 1972. *Resettlement Policy and Services for Disabled People*. London: HMSO.

Harris, A. I., Cox, E. & Smith, C. R. W. 1971. *Handicapped and Impaired in Great Britain*, Part 1. London: HMSO.

Mair Report. 1972. *Report of Sub Committee of the Standing Medical Advisory Committee, Scottish Health Services Council on Medical Rehabilitation*. Edinburgh: HMSO.

Richardson, S. A., Hastorf, A. H. & Dornbusch, S. M. 1964. Effects of physical disability on a child's description of himself. *Child Development*, **35**, 893–907.

Tomlinson Committee. 1943. *Report of the Interdepartmental Committee on Rehabilitation and Resettlement of Disabled Persons*. Cmnd. 6415. London: HMSO.

Ward, P. R. 1974. *Proposals for a Questionnaire for use in the 1976 Census of Residential Accommodation, DHSS Dependency Project Report No. 1*. Private Communication.

Warren, M. E. 1974. The need for rehabilitation. *Update*, May, p. 1286.

Chapter 2

Clarke, A. D. & Clarke, A. 1976. *Early Experience: Myth and Evidence*. London: Open Books.

Deacon, J. J. 1974. *Tongue Tied*. London: National Society for Mentally Handicapped Children.

Department of Health, Education and Welfare, Institutes of Health, and Department of Labour. 1973. *President's Committee on the Employment of the Handicapped*. Washington: US Government Printing Office.

Dillard, J. 1972. *Black English*. New York: Random House.

Dobbing, J. & Sands, J. 1973. Quantitative growth and development of the human brain. *Arch. Disease in Childhood*, **48**, 758–67.

European Coal & Steel Community, European Economic Community, European Atomic Energy Commission. 1975. *Report on the Development of the Social Situation in the Community in 1974*. Luxemburg:

Office for Official Publications of the European Community.

Home Office. 1968. *Urban Aid Programme: Circular of Guidance, No. 225/68*. London: HMSO.

National Child Development Study / Kellmer Pringle, M. L., Butler, N. R. & Davie, R. 1966. *11,000 Seven-Year-Olds*. London: Longman, Green.

National Children's Bureau / Wedge, P. & Prosser, H. 1973. *Born to Fail?* London: Arrow Special.

Seebohm Report. 1968. *Report of the Committee on Local Authority and Allied Personal Social Services*. Cmnd. 3703. London: HMSO.

Skeels, H. M. & Dye, H. B. 1939. A study of the effects of differential stimulation on mentally retarded children. *Proc. Am. Ass. Mental Deficiency*, **44**, 114–36.

Taylor, O. L. 1973. Sociolinguistics and the practice of speech pathology. *Rehabilitation Record*, May/June, 14–17.

Williamson, J. A. 1971. *A Varied Language*. New York: Holt, Rinehart & Winston.

Chapter 3

Bower, T. E. R. 1974. *Development in Infancy*. San Francisco: W. H. Freeman.

Broomfield, A. M. 1967. Guidance to parents of deaf children—a perspective. *Br. J. Disorders of Communication*, **2**, 112–23.

Chomsky, C. & Chomsky, N. 1965. *Aspects of the Theory of Syntax*. Cambridge: MIT Press.

Clarke & Clarke, op. cit.

Colton, E. & Parnell, M. 1967. From Hungary: the Peto Method. *Special Education*, **56**, No. 4.

Craig, W. N. 1968. Language learning in deaf children. In *Proceedings of Institute for Parents of Preschool Hearing Impaired Children and Professional Personnel*. Pennsylvania: Chester County Board of School Directors.

Easson, W. M. 1969. *The Severely Disturbed Adolescent*. New York: International Universities Press.

Furth, H. G. 1966. *Thinking Without Language*. New York: Free Press.

Inhelder, B. & Piaget, J. 1958. *The Growth of Logical Thinking from Childhood to Adolescence*. New York: Basic Books.

Jaehnig, W. J. 1974. *The Mentally Handicapped and their Families*. Final Report, 2 vols. Colchester: U. of Essex.

McGraw, M. B. 1940. Neural motivation as exemplified by bladder control. *Journal of Paediatrics*, **16**, 580–90.

Meadow, K. P. & Meadow, L. 1971. Changing role perceptions for parents of handicapped children. *Exceptional Children*, **38**, 21–37.

Myklebust, H. R. 1964. *Psychology of Deafness*. 2nd edn. New York: Grune & Stratton.

Northcott, Winifred H. 1971. *The Hearing Impaired Child in a Regular Classroom*. Washington: A. G. Bell Association.

Parsons, T. & Bales, R. F. 1955. *Familiy Socialization and Interaction Process*. New York: Free Press.

Reynell, J. 1973. Planning treatment programmes for pre-school children. In *Assessment for Learning in the Mentally Handicapped*, ed. P. Mittler. London: Churchill.

Rutter, M., Tizzard, J. & Whitmore, K. 1970. *Education, Health and Behaviour*. London: Longman.

Schaefer, E. S. 1965. A configurational analysis of children's reports of parent behavior. In *Contemporary Issues in Developmental Psychology*, ed. N. S. Endler. New York: Holt, Rinehart & Winston.

Walker, M. 1976. *The Revised Makaton Vocabulary*. London: Royal Assoc. in aid of the Deaf and Dumb.

Wrightstone, J. W., Aronow, M. S. & Moskowitz, B. L. 1963. *Developing Reading Test Norms for Deaf Children*. New York: Harcourt, Brace & World.

Chapter 4

Anderson, Elizabeth. 1973. *The Disabled Schoolchild: A Study of Integration in Primary Schools*. London: Methuen.

Cratty, B. J. & Sams, T. A. 1968. *The Body-Image of Blind Children*. New York: American Foundation for the Blind.

Davis, R. B. 1967. *The Changing Curriculum: Mathematics*. Washington: Association for Supervision and Curriculum.

Department of Health and Social Security. 1976. *Prevention and Health: Everybody's Business*. London: HMSO.

Gunzburg, H. C. & Gunzburg, A. L. 1973. *Mental Handicap and Physical Environment*. London: Baillière Tindall.

Holman, R. 1973. Poverty: consensus and alternatives. *Br. J. Social Work*, **3/4**, 431–46.

Kennedy, J. F. *A National Plan to Combat Mental Retardation—A Statement of Need*. Washington: Department of Health, Education and Welfare (851J/Pr. 35.8: M52/M52). See also President's Panel on Mental Retardation. 1962. *Report to the President: A proposed program for national action to combat mental retardation*. Washington: US Government Printing Office.

Longmate, N. 1974. *The Workhouse: A Social History*. London: Temple Smith.

Miller, E. J. & Gwynne, G. V. 1973. *A Life Apart*. London: Tavistock Publications.

Rutter, M. & Madge, N. 1976. *Cycles of Disadvantage*. London: Heinemann.

Thorpe, L. P. & Johnson, V. 1962. *Child Psychology and Development*. 3rd edn. New York: The Ronald Press.

Veness, T. 1961. *School Leavers: Their Aspirations and Expectations*. London: Methuen.

Chapter 5

Council of Ministers, Council of Europe. 1972. Resolution AP(72)5 on the planning and equipment of buildings with a view to making them more accessible to the physically handicapped.

Dexter, L. A. 1958. A social theory of mental deficiency. *Am. J. Mental Deficiency*, **63**, 920–8.

Dubot, G., Mirot, F. & Salmon, A. 1971. Placement and adjustment in a normal factory. Practical aspects. In *Proc. of European Symposium on Occupational Rehabilitation and Placement of the Disabled*. Luxemburg: Commission of European Communities.

Festinger, L. 1957. *A Theory of Cognitive Dissonance*. New York: Harper & Row.

Harris, *et al.*, op. cit.

Goldsmith, S. 1976. *Designing for the Disabled*. 3rd edn. London: RIBA Publications.

Johnson, G. S., & Johnson, R. H. 1973. Paraplegics in Scotland: a survey of employment and facilities. *Br. J. Social Work*, **3**, 19–38.

Lewin, K. 1951. *Field Theory in Social Science*. New York: Harper & Row.

Linduska, N. 1947. *My Polio Post*. Chicago: Pellegrini & Cudahy.

Mattingly, S. 1974. Rehabilitation today. *Update*, April, 1129–36.

Tomlinson Committee, op. cit.

Chapter 6

Bromley, D. B. 1966. *The Psychology of Human Ageing*. Harmondsworth: Penguin.

Clement, F., Cendron, H. & Housset, P. 1968. Le vieillissement différential d'une population ouvrière dans la region parisienne. *Bull. Inserm.*, **23**, 889–920.

Harris, *et al.*, op. cit.

Ho, M. T. & Quinot, E. 1974. Apparition et aggravation de la surdité dans une population exposée au bruit. *Cahiers de Notes Documentaires*, **75**, Note 895, 74–5.

Ledermann, S. 1961. In *Les Limites de la Vie Humaine*, ed. A. Sauvy. Paris: Hachette.

Naylor, G. & Harwood, E. 1975. Old dogs, new tricks: age and ability. *New Psychology*, **1**, 29–33.

Savage, R. D., *et al.* 1973. *Intellectual Function in the Aged*. London: Methuen.

Shanas, E. 1970. What's new in old age? In *Ageing in Contemporary Society*, ed. E. Shanas. Beverly Hills/London: Sage Publications.

Wedderburn, D. 1967. How adequate are our cash benefits? *New Society*, 12 October, 263.

Welford, A. T. 1958. *Ageing and Human Skills*. Oxford: OUP.

Wisner, A. 1975. Age and marks of life. Paper read at International Conference on the Older Worker: 25 Years' Research in Retrospect and Prospects for the Future. Cardiff: University of Wales, September.

Chapter 7

Bayley, M. 1973. *Mental Handicap and Community Care: A Study of Mentally Handicapped People in Sheffield*. London: Routledge & Kegan Paul.

Department of Employment. 1973. *The Quota Scheme for Disabled People*. London: HMSO.

Goffman, E. 1968. *Stigma: Notes on the Management of Spoiled Identity*. Harmondsworth: Penguin.

Kutner, B., Wilkins, C. & Yarrow, P. R. 1952. Verbal attitudes and overt behavior involving racial prejudice. *J. of Abnormal and Social Psychology*, **47**, 649–52.

La Piere, R. T. 1934. Attitudes versus actions. *Social Forces*, **13**, 230–7.

Large, P. 1973. *Memorandum of the Association of Disabled Professionals on the Consultative Document 'The Quota Scheme for Disabled People' issued by the DOE, May 1973*. London: Association of Disabled Professionals.

Rokeach, M. 1968. Attitudes. In *International Encyclopedia of the Social Sciences*, vol. 1. New York: Collier Macmillan.

Schein, J. D. & Delk, M. T. 1974. *The Deaf Population of the United States*. Silver Spring, Md: National Association of the Deaf.

Townsend, P., ed. 1976. *Disability Rights Handbook for 1977*. London: The Disability Alliance.

Index